Seeing yourself through the eyes of Jesus

Oneness Personified

Freely I receive
Freely I give

Nelson

Christine Nelson

© 2014 by Christine Nelson. All rights reserved.

No part of this book may be reproduced, stored in a retrieval system, or transmitted by any means without the written permission of the author.

Scripture quotations are taken from the New American Standard Bible (NASB) unless denoted otherwise.

ISBN-10: 1505430046
ISBN-13: 978-1505430042

Because of the dynamic nature of the internet, any web addresses or links contained in this book may have changed since publication and may no longer be valid.

Contents

Dedication..		v
Acknowledgements.........................		vii
Introduction....................................		ix
How to read this book....................		xvii
Day 1:	Jesus – Light of the world	21
Day 2:	Jesus – The Tabernacle	33
Day 3:	Jesus – The Liberator / Door	47
Day 4:	Jesus – A Child	63
Day 5:	Jesus – Son of God	71
Day 6:	Jesus – King of kings	89
Day 7:	Jesus – Bread of Life	111
Day 8:	Jesus – The Great High Priest	129
Day 9:	Jesus – The Healer	143
Day 10:	Jesus – The Prophet	153
Day 11:	Jesus – The Teacher	163
Day 12:	Jesus – Lion of Judah	173
Day 13:	Jesus – Author and Finisher	185

Dedication

This book is dedicated to my first love Jesus; the lover of my soul. Many years ago, when I came to know the Lord, it was the life of Jesus that completely captivated me.

The more I gazed upon Him the more I became enraptured by His unconditional love for me, His devotion, His selflessness, His passion for people changed me forever. This was the first time I had seen such love. I fell in love with the One who loved me first in all my sin, shame, guilt, BUT in spite of, called me to be His own.

For the first time I was being loved for who I was but with a glimpse of all I could be and become in Him. Such love was too lofty for me to imagine. The more I seek to grow in Him the more I have become intoxicated by His love, leaving me hungering and thirsting for more of Him.

Christine Nelson

I enjoy being with Him like no other, for I know He knows my heart intimately and adores me. To be like Him is my only desire, to reflect Him is my only goal, to draw others to Him is my only plan.

See yourself through the eyes of Jesus and let Him show you who you really are. For as He is, so are you!

Acknowledgements

I wish to express my deepest appreciation to my husband, for his patience and support. To my boys Kobi and Kristian for their encouragement.

To Torema Thompson for her tireless and wholehearted help in preparing this book internally.

To Ann Burke who designed the best book cover ever! Thank you so much Ann.

To my friends Kika Ashanike and Nicole Dennis, for their help with editing, encouragement and support.

To all the partners of Christine Nelson Ministries, thank you for dreaming with me. Thank you for your support and prayers.

Introduction

Jesus has many names. Each name describes His character.

A person's name, when given, is significant of a spiritual truth. The name you carry is a reflection of the mandate God has given you to walk out on Earth. Interpreting the name, we interpret the nature and the message behind the name.

> **"and to him Abraham apportioned a tenth part of everything. He is first, by translation of his name, king of righteousness, and then he is also king of Salem, that is, king of peace."**
> (Hebrews 7:2)

Christine Nelson

"By translation of His name"...the word translation means meaning. Reiterating the meaning implied his character.

If **"as Jesus is, so are we in this world"**... (1 John 4:17b), then truly we can see who we are by looking at JESUS through His names. The question is, who is Jesus?

He is the exact representation of our Father. He is our divine pattern. He is all we need to be; all that we can be. To know Him is to know who we are. The knowledge of Him affords us to be all we can be as Ambassadors of Christ. The more we see ourselves through His eyes the more we will walk, talk and carry ourselves like Him. We will walk in complete oneness of mind, will and emotions as true representatives and true expressions of Him.

Seeing yourself through the eyes of Jesus

Seeing ourselves through the eyes of Jesus will help us see ourselves from His perspective; not our own nor any other worldly viewpoint. Jesus' perspective enables us to see that we are made in His image. His view gives us a Heaven to Earth perspective which brings healing and direction. This will empower us to become all that He says we are and to walk in our complete identity.

Again describing this oneness - that is, whatever He is not, the same is true of us (His followers). Consequently, the opposite is true; whatever He is - so are we (His children). Furthermore, whatever belongs to Jesus, is also ours.

Below is a table that illustrates this truth; from the Father → to the Son → to His children.

Father	The Son	Children
Father judges. *John 8:16*	The Son judges. *John 8:16*	Children judge. *1Cor. 6:1-5*
God is light. *1John 1:5*	The Son is light of the world. *John 8:12, John 12:46*	Children live in the light of God's presence. *Matt. 5:14,*
Father teaches. *John 8:28*	The Son teaches. *John 8:28*	Children teach. *Acts 5:42, 1Tim. 3:2, 1Tim. 4:11*
Father gave His Son *John 3:16*	The Son gave His life *John 10:11*	Children lay down their lives for one another *1John 3:16*
Father is perfect. *Matt. 5:48*	The Son is perfect. *Matt.5:48*	Children are made perfect in their weakness. *2 Cor.12:9, Col.3:10*

From this table, you can see that there is a clear pattern of the Father's actions, Jesus' actions and the actions of His children. This illustrates the unity and oneness shared between God the Father, Jesus and His children through the power of the Holy Spirit. Jesus is the image of God in human form, God simply wants His people to bear His image (exact representation, true likeness) of Him[1].

Jesus has given us the power of attorney to be an expression of Himself; to demonstrate the same authority and power, to do His works and even greater works.

Here's another example of some parallels.

---

[1] Taken from the book 'Walking in Oneness - Taking the Father by the Hand'. (First book in the Walking in Oneness Series).

Jesus	His disciples
He is the Son of God	We become sons of God
He is Great Physician and Healer	We will lay hands on the sick and they will recover
He is the light of the World	We are the light in the darkness
He is living water	Out of our bellies will flow living waters
He is the chief cornerstone	We are living stones

There are 3 kinds of people reading this book....

1. Those who do not believe
2. Those who have believed but have not experienced this as a reality in their lives.
3. Those who believe this truth and more and more this is their lifestyle.

My prayer is that as you read this book your faith will be built and you will not only dream of

Seeing yourself through the eyes of Jesus

the possibilities, but you will experience the life Jesus intended for you as your reality. As we embark on this journey, of changing our perspective, let us endeavour to SEE THROUGH THE EYES OF JESUS.

How to read this book

This book can be read in thirteen days. Each day highlights a name of Jesus that we will explore. Reading all 13 will inevitably bring you on a journey of finding your true self in HIM.

The number thirteen in BIBLICAL HEBREW is the bonding of many into one. For example: - Jesus had 12 disciples and He made 13. Judas died and Matthias replaced Him and Paul was added which still remained 13 apostles. It was this group of men that God used as One man to turned the world upside down. Like the Apostles, may the Lord use you to turn your world upside down as you become an expression of Christ Himself.

The number 13 is recognized by the Jews as a time of spiritual maturity. It is usually at age 13 that Hebrew children have their Bar/Bat Mitzvah (son /daughter of commandment). The Bar/Bat Mitzvah is the beginning of the completion of one's purpose in being born, to serve God. A child is trained from birth about how to serve God. At Bar/Bat Mitzvah, they are "given wings" and become responsible for their own actions by following the scriptures.

My prayer is that as you read and engage with all 13 days, you will gain wings to fly. Every dead weight will lift in Jesus' name. Each chapter carries a facet of Jesus that will bring you into maturity or a position that is recognized. At a Bar/Bat Mitzvah there is a time of declaring who you are, likewise, at the end of each chapter there is a declaration. Speak out that declaration until you believe it as your own.

This book is geared to establish your identity in Christ. It is noted in the book of John that Jesus described His identity 13 ways. Our identity is the fundamentals of who we really are because without His identity there is no true power. To embrace our true identity in Him, everything is possible!

My prayer is that, by the end of this book you will walk in His identity wholeheartedly. You will rise to a mirror image of Jesus as your own. Since **"as a man thinks in his heart so is he"** (Proverbs 23:7), may the Lord Jesus renew our minds so we can WALK IN ONENESS with who He says we are and begin to SEE OURSELVES THROUGH THE EYES OF JESUS!

Day 1:

Jesus – Light of the world

> *"For with you is the fountain of life; in your light we see light."*
> *(Psalm 36:9)*

When Jesus was on Earth everywhere He went He brought such light that demons fled. Religious spirits were challenged, ailing bodies recovered. If you can, imagine what happens when a light switch is turned off, darkness takes over. When we do the reverse by turning the light on, darkness runs in an instant. I perceive this as a Heaven to Earth reality in that, when light turns up anything that is representative of Heaven is made manifest. Psalm 36:9 expresses this beautifully... **"For with You is the Fountain of life, in Your light we**

see light." My view of this is that our true light cannot manifest unless we have the Real Light of the world on the inside of us. By seeing through His light we see all that we are.

I have reached out to unbelievers, with the intention to encourage them to give their lives to the Lord. A repetitive response I can recall is, the need to sort self out first. Sometimes we fail to realize that we can do nothing without His light on the inside of us. We cannot see without His light. John 8:12;

Jesus said "I am the light of the world he who follows Me shall by no means walk in darkness."

The Light of the world came to deliver us from the darkness of sin and bondage. When the Light comes and resides in us, the light of life shines within man by the inner sense of life to deliver man from sin. John 1:4-5;

In Him was life, and the life was the light of men and the light shines in the darkness, and the darkness did not overcome it.

The Light came to enlighten every man, the Light reveals truth. To live in the light is to live a transparent life being open and honest; willingness to be taught and to be corrected, hence no inhibition to speak truth. It is only by speaking, walking, living and facing the truth that we can be free. When we become fearful and put up barricades around our hearts, it prevents us from being open and truthful, we will live in bondage and we will not live in His light but in darkness. People are drawn to openness, or as I often remind myself openness breeds openness.

Openness makes room for His truth, light and ultimately His freedom.

The blind man was living in darkness, his eyes had been in darkness from birth. Likewise, many who have not given their lives to Jesus are also living in darkness. They must invite Jesus in by faith so that their lives can be illuminated and so that they can truly know who they are and where they are going.

Jesus Himself told the Pharisees that they did not know Him because they did not know where Jesus came from and where He was going. It is only through Jesus illuminating our lives (our eyes) that we will be able to truly see, like the blind man whose eyes were then opened by Jesus (the Light). You see **"satan has blinded the thoughts of unbelievers"** (2 Corinthians 4:4). For unbelievers to see, the illumination of the Gospel of the glory of Christ must shine on them

Seeing yourself through the eyes of Jesus

to **"open their eyes, to turn them from darkness to light and from the authority of satan to God"** (Acts 26:18).

By faith in Jesus' words to go and wash his eyes, the blind man was restored. In the same way, for us to move from darkness to light, we too need to believe Jesus' words and act upon them. His light directs our path, Jesus is the lamp unto our feet. His light illuminates our minds and orders our steps.

So, if you are reading this book and you do not know Jesus as Lord, as the light that lives in you, I would love to give you the opportunity to give your life to Him. If this is your heart, pray this prayer with all your HEART.

Dear God, I come before you as a sinner. I am sorry for my sins and the self-centred way I have lived my life. I need your forgiveness. I believe that Jesus is the Son of God who came and died and resurrected for me, so I can live a life of light - revelation, transparency and to be full of God Himself. You said in Romans 10:9 that if we confess with our mouths and believe in our hearts that God raised Jesus from the dead we shall be saved. Today I confess Jesus as the Lord of my life, my heart, my soul and according to Your word I am now saved. AMEN!! HALLELUJAH!!

How can believers be a light?

In Matthew 6:22 it says;

"the eye is the lamp of the body; so then if your eye is clear your whole body will be full of light."

This scripture is so powerful, because it is telling us directly to watch what we put before our eyes. Your eyes determine how much light you have in your body. The reverse is also true; if you want your body to be full of HIS light then focus on those things that will. Philippians 4:8 puts it this way;

> ***"Whatever is true, whatever is honourable, whatever is right, whatever is pure, whatever is lovely, whatever is of good repute, if there is any excellence and worthy of praise dwell on these things."***

These are categories of things that we should focus on or behold. Remember whatever we behold we become. Focus on the things that carry His light and expect your body to become full of His light.

Light (revelation) helps you to move forward. When we look at the world many are in various types of bondages; like witchcraft, many profess to be witches as a skill, many are into Satanism, pornography and yet there are many believers who are afraid of reaching out in love because of fear.

Recently, I was in a store buying some supplies, when I instantly knew that the cashier who was serving me, was into Satanism of some kind. I instantly smelt the spirit of death. Fear gripped me and I immediately began to pray in tongues in my mind.

As I was praying in tongues I heard the Lord say to me "you are afraid". He reminded me of how He sees this man and how I needed to see him. I changed my defensive response and rested in the Father's love and smiled at the man and showed him kindness. I was convicted by our Father's love towards Him and since then I have purposed in my heart to go the extra mile, rather than cowering in fear but to remind myself I am the light of Christ coming into every dark place.

The Bible says; **"Perfect love cast out all fear"**. I believe as we continue to receive the love of God we too will be able to look beyond the practices of these groups and see their hearts. They are seeking to fill their emptiness but have been disillusioned by seeking it out in the wrong places. I believe that if we capture the heart of the Father, by demonstrating the love of God, they can be set free.

So how can we become a light in a dark place? Sometimes we have to go into those dark places and be the light and minister. I heard of one friend who went with some leaders of her church to a gay bar to sing songs of God's love. I heard of one ministry that went to a fair that was promoting new agers and witchcraft and they went as children of God and prophesied, prayed for people, in Jesus name, and healed many.

When we understand that we are the light and we have a responsibility, we understand that when we walk into a dark room and switch the light on, darkness flees. We have great power as the light of God, so instead of hiding under a bushel it is time to be a light.

...Father, in Your first words, You spoke to the darkness to become light. We too cry out **"Let there be light"** when we are perplexed by what to do. Let light illuminate our minds by giving us revelation of who we are and to see ourselves in YOUR light....Let there be light in our families, in our neighbourhoods, in our place of work, in our nation.

Declaration

Jesus is the Light of the world. Because I follow Him, by obeying His words, I will live in the light as He illuminates my path, bringing understanding and revelation to my mind. As Jesus brings light into my life, I too seek to set the captives free by teaching the words of Jesus. I seek to be an example of Jesus, so that His light, which dwells within me, will draw others out of darkness, into His wonderful light and break the chains of bondage that have perverted their minds with lies. We declare let there be LIGHT, ILLUMINATION, REVELATION...

Day 2:

Jesus – The Tabernacle

> *"Do you not know that you are the temple of God and that the Spirit of God dwells in you? If any man destroys the temple of God, God will destroy him, for the temple of God is holy, and that is what you are.(1 Corinthians 3:16-17)*

The question is not, 'where is GOD?' That is because, you are the temple/ tabernacle in whom He dwells. The tabernacle is a place where God wanted to demonstrate His union with man. The word 'tabernacle' means 'tent of meeting'. It's where God met and interacted with His people. 1 Corinthians 6:16 says we are His temple, suggesting that as we become children of God, the

Father sees us as holy and hence comes and dwells within us. How awesome is that? Hallelujah!

In the Old Testament, the Lord did not dwell within His people but among His people. Today we have this amazing privilege to be One with Christ as He resides in us. The question we have to ask is why? By observation we can see that an inside out job is far more effective when we understand how it works. Jesus Himself said *"if you will abide in me and I in you, you will be able to ask for whatever you wish and it will be granted"* (John 15: 7). So often we are asking but we are not abiding in Him...

Often we focus on the outward - how we look, what we wear and so on - as more important than what is going on, on the inside. Jesus said in John 14:23 *"If a man love me, he will keep my words: and my Father will love him, and we will come unto him, and make our abode*

with him." Jesus becomes our tabernacle as we keep His words and obey them. When we do this He promises to come dwell with or tabernacle with us and to make Himself known to us. You see, obedience from the heart to the Lord, is an open invitation for the Lord to come and make His home in you. Colossians 3:3;

"For as far as this world is concerned you have died, and your (new real) life is hidden with Christ in God."

We need to find our new real life; it is in the Holy of Holies where Christ dwells in you and I (assuming you have made Jesus LORD).

The reality of this tabernacle is twofold. In our obedience Jesus comes and dwell within us. Equally as we remain dead to this world and alive to Christ we are hidden with Christ in God. The ark that God instructed Noah to build in Genesis 8 is a typology of the tabernacle. When we look at the benefits of staying in the ark we will understand the need to abide in Christ: - The ark provided a covering, a shelter, it sustained, brought refuge and rest. The ark was also divided into three layers as the tabernacle. The layers represented 3 tiers the outer court, inner court and the Holy of Holies. Each tier has its own function. If we were to see ourselves in these three dimensions, like the tabernacle or the ark, we would then see on a larger scale the scope that can be had through functioning from the inside out pattern in all things.

You are a spirit being not a human being

Failure to embrace that you are a spirit that lives in a body who has a soul is to embrace a false identity.

Like the Triune God we serve, we too have been made in His image as tripartite beings. We are body, soul and spirit. The body is the outer court of the tabernacle, the soul is the inner court (the mind, the will and the emotions) and the spirit man is the Holy of Holies. Those who operate solely from the body can find themselves crippled by insecurity because they are trying to fit a worldly standard of how to look. When the compliments or attention being sought, are not received many begin to use their bodies in seductive ways.

When we reside in the mind, there is a dependence on what is logical or makes sense. The temptation is to then reason away the voice of the Lord because we are looking for logic, but our God is not logical. So often we can find ourselves derailed and failing to walk in obedience, which eventually steals our faith.

When we are led by our wills we can become overworked, disgruntled, burnt out, and discouraged as we are driven to work hard, showing great tenacity and diligence. However, most times we have forgotten to seek the Lord to find out what His divine strategy is, to accomplish His divine plan. Instead, we are driven by law and works rather than the grace that comes from being in an intimate relationship with Christ; inquiring of Him every step of the way and doing as HE leads.

Another facet we can be led by is our emotions. Our emotions are ways the body, or the mind, may speak to us. The mind may tell us that it cannot do something and it can make us feel inadequate. Though our emotions are important, if we are led by them, it could lead us down destructive patterns. It is important to acknowledge your emotions by using the Word of God as a mirror to direct them.

Ultimately, it is important to learn how to express your emotions, surrender your will and declutter your mind so that they will be under Christ's authority. If we fail to do this, we could feel like a roller coaster going up and down moving and going around in circles but going nowhere... While those who are led by the Spirit are always looking to the Spirit for direction, hence they have tunnel vision. Many times the mind, the will and emotions and the body will try to derail our focus by way of distraction. This can only be dealt with through entering and dwelling in the rest of knowing the heart, mind-set and love of God.

Seeing the Holy of Holies through Jesus' eyes

The Holy of Holies gives us a glimpse of Jesus being our life. As believers we must move beyond the veil. Ephesians 2:13-18;

> *"But now in Christ Jesus you who once were far off have been brought near by the blood of Christ. For He Himself is our peace, who has made both one, and has broken down the middle wall of separation, having abolished in His*

> *flesh the enmity, that is, the law of commandments contained in ordinances, so as to create in Himself one new man from the two, thus making peace, and that He might reconcile them both to God in one body through the cross, thereby putting to death the enmity. And He came and preached peace to you who were afar off and to those who were near. For through Him we both have access by one Spirit to the Father."*

According to this scripture, Jesus sacrificed Himself so that coming behind the veil would not only be possible but accessible to us; behind the veil is Heaven itself. Hebrews 10:19-22;

> *"Therefore, brethren, having boldness to enter the Holiest by the blood of Jesus, by a new and living way which*

He consecrated for us, through the veil, that is, His flesh, and having a High Priest over the house of God, let us draw near with a true heart in full assurance of faith, having our hearts sprinkled from an evil conscience and our bodies washed with pure water."

Again an appeal to us not to stop at the outer court being happy we are saved but to go further and deeper. Knowing that the blood of Jesus has set us apart to enter the Holy of Holies where God dwells. This is where we are transformed. This is where we are saturated with His presence and power. This is where we are cleansed and sanctified. This is where we are rejuvenated and empowered. This is where we engage with the Triune God face to face. This is home. Every good Daddy wants their children to come home.

In this heavenly place is where you can ask those questions, and you are given direct answers that will leave you forever changed. The inside out principle of going into the SECRET PLACE, the THRONE ROOM, HEAVEN itself to commune with God is where you fight your battles from and where you find all you need to be victorious on Earth. Let us acknowledge once and for all, that we are the tabernacle the dwelling place of God. Then let us no longer settle for the outer courts (body) nor the inner courts only (soul, mind, will and emotions) but to boldly enter the Holy of Holies (spirit) where Jesus has given us access, through His sacrificial death.

How then should we treat the tabernacle?
The Lord Jesus showed such passion and zeal for the temple when He whipped the people out who were marketing there. We are God's temple (1 Corinthians 3:16-17), hence the same zeal that Jesus demonstrated to us, by clearing the temple

with fervency and honour, is the same attitude we must have firstly towards clearing and honouring the temple of our hearts. We are to ensure our heart is clean, pure and that sin is radically dealt with.

The Bible says we should **"watch over our hearts because it is the wellspring of life;"** (Proverbs 4:23). It is out of our hearts that His life flows. As we seek to keep our hearts pure we are being prepared to meet our bridegroom because He said the **"pure in heart will see God"** (Matthew 5:8).

Secondly, this is the same attitude we must have towards those who become a dwelling place for the Lord of Lords. We must ensure that we do not turn a blind eye to sin in the lives of others, instead be sure to come alongside and encourage, edify and exhort so as to prevent any hardness of heart.

Lessons from the tabernacle
1. Our Father is an inside out God.
2. We are all valuable to God... None is better... He is no respecter of persons.
3. We can't live on yesterday's fire... He sets us alight - we are responsible to keep His fire going.
4. He remembers our sin no more. You are cleansed because you have been forgiven.

How do we step into the realm of Heaven?
When we have the revelation that we are the tabernacle where God dwells, it becomes a reality for us to enter. Revelations 4:1 gives us an open invitation to enter through the open door...

Begin by envisioning this open door. What do you see? Whatever you see write it down. We are not just hearers of the word we are doers. As doers of the word we experience the reality of the word.

Seeing yourself through the eyes of Jesus

Genesis 28:10-22 and John 1:52 tell us about Jacob's dream, where he saw a ladder that came from Heaven; he saw angels ascending and descending. Jesus announced to Nathanael in John 1:51 that He is that ladder. So, therefore we need to understand that He is the way in.

I was in the kitchen one day minding my own business cooking, when the Lord said to me, "if you were to go to Jamaica how would you go?" I replied, "I would need a Jamaican passport." He then inquired of me "How would you get to Heaven if you were to come? I thought for a moment... and whispered sheepishly "a passport?" He then asked, "Who is your passport?" I thought thank you Daddy that was my hint so I almost shouted with great confidence, "JESUS!"

So you see by revelation Daddy God was revealing to me these scriptures. Jesus is the

Ladder the WAY in. See yourself going up that ladder and enter in that open door.

Declaration

Father, You call me holy and you deemed it a privilege to come and dwell within me; an initiative of how close You want to be with me. Thank You, You are a God of many patterns. I declare that I will not settle for an outer court relationship nor an inner court relationship, but I will come boldly to the Holy of Holies because You have already given me the keys through the blood of Jesus. I have access into Heaven, my home, what an honour. I choose to come behind the veil because the blood of Jesus has cleansed me and sanctified me. I declare I live from my spirit because I am the tabernacle of God. Only from this perspective can I have authority over my soul and my body. I choose to honour my temple and all of the other temples around me because you are no respecter of persons.

Day 3:
Jesus – The Liberator / Door

> *The Spirit of the Lord God is upon me, because the Lord has anointed me to bring good news to the afflicted. He has sent me to bind up the broken-hearted to proclaim liberty to captives and freedom to prisoners. (Isaiah 61:1)*

A Liberator is someone who sets people free. The very function of a Liberator implies that we were imprisoned, stifled, enslaved, bonded, oppressed, or hindered in order for us to be set free. Jesus said to the Jews who believed Him;

"If you abide in my word you are truly my disciples and you will know the

TRUTH and the truth will set you free." (John 8:31)

Jesus was speaking to believers. He was instructing them on how to walk in their God given freedom, by living out the word. As they did, they would experience the revelatory truth of the word in their lives.

Pulling down strongholds from the mind

The Jews then and some now, have not believed the truth of Jesus being the Messiah, the Son of God. This lack of belief in who He is, is bondage or strongholds on the mind. Inevitably, God the Father sent Jesus to deliver us from the bondage of religion and a wrong way of thinking. Egypt is a classic example of the world portrayed and the bondage under satan's rule (John12:31, Ephesians 2:2). The bondage of God's people prevented them from fulfilling the purpose for which God created them. The enemy brought God's people into slavery

Seeing yourself through the eyes of Jesus

where they were being ruled by the spirit of Pharaoh and Mammon (a spirit of oppression) rather than God Himself. God's goal is to liberate His people from slavery and persecution and to bring them to Himself at the mountain of God so that He might infuse them with Himself. He told Moses to bring His people to the Mountain of God after he liberated them (Exodus 3:12b) so He could make them His personal treasure, a Kingdom of priests, and a holy nation.

Today the call is the same, God is calling us to the Mountain of God to the highest point in Him. The scripture (Exodus 19:1-25) highlights 3 tiers to the mountain. Moses was at the top of the mountain, Joshua was further down from Moses while the people of Israel were almost at the foot of the mountain. When we assess these three levels of attainment, truth and revelation determined the height desired. The people of Israel, though they prepared themselves to meet with God, were afraid to go any further up the mountain but relied on Moses to go and fetch the word from the Lord instead. Where we are in our relationship with God is not up to God but up to us. His word promises if we would **"Draw near to God and He will draw near to you"** (James 4:8). What will it take for you to come up higher?

I believe for the Israelites it was fear, because the enemy always uses fear to imprison. Sometimes we can refuse to step into the freedom that God gives through His manifest presence. In His presence there is fullness of joy, transformation, revelation; today He extends to us the same invitation. Revelations 4:1; "Come up here and I will show you the things to come." The Lord has given us an open invitation to come up higher; to be wholly filled with His presence and power to the fullness of God (Ephesians 3:19). Let us not to not tarry, but relentlessly pursue Him...

Religion is a prison- choose relationship and be free

Our Father works through relationship. Religion operates in methods and formulas rather than the leading of the Holy Spirit. Religion leaves you asking questions, wishing you could change... a relationship with Jesus empowers you to change things. Religion stifles the Holy Spirit's power, while relationship sees the Holy Spirit as the power to heal, deliver, and to raise the dead. I believe a right relationship with God is always growing and developing in transparency, intimacy, knowing His role and knowing His heart towards you.

There is a freedom in our relationship with Daddy God that lets us know undoubtedly that we are loved unconditionally. His love does not control but gives us the ability to choose. When you are in a relationship where you are valued and trusted to make right choices, it inevitably enables us to choose Him or what is best for the relationship.

Religion on the other hand, is motivated by fear and so it resorts to phrases like; you must, you have to, if you don't this will happen... It perceives God as big God with a stick chastising you to do what is right. When we are in a right relationship with God we see Him empowering us to do what is right.

Jesus our access point to everything

Jesus is THE Door NOT a DOOR, The WAY not A WAY. The world would like to feed us various forms of doctrine to cause us to compromise. John 10:1b says; **"anyone who climbs up some other WAY, he is a thief and a robber."** There is only one WAY to freedom it is not through allah, buddah, hindi gods, new age, witchcraft, manipulation, deceit or lies. To attempt to combine God's way with any of these ways is reasoning, which leads to folly, deception and perversion. Jesus is THE only Door that can lead us into true freedom.

Jesus being the Door suggest that when we enter through Him there is a freedom to go anywhere in Him. His mind, His heart, His direction, His truth, His ways, His life. In verse 9 of John 10 it says,

> *"I am the door; if anyone enters through me, he shall be saved and shall go in and go out and shall find pasture."*

What does Jesus mean when He says going in and out and find pasture?" Jesus being our pasture is in Psalm 23:1-2;

> *"The Lord is my Shepherd; I shall not want. He makes me down to lie down in green pastures: He leads me beside the still waters."*

We can only experience Jesus as our pastures when we embrace Him as our shepherd (our guide, our protector, our provider) we will lie in His rest and He will be our food, anything we need to satisfy us, as He is our pastures.

Jesus is that Door to prevent the thief from coming in to steal, kill and destroy. The Door that will protect the sheep from the devourer; so we fear no evil. Christ is the Door for God's elect not only as protector or preventer but the Door for which we can go in and the Door for which God's chosen people can go out. Doors lead you into what lies ahead. Jesus is also the Door that leads us out of bondage like the law. Galatians 4:3-5;

> ***"So we [Jewish Christians] also, when we were minors, were kept like slaves under [the rules of the Hebrew ritual and subject to] the elementary teachings of a system of external observations and regulations. But when the proper time had fully come, God***

sent His Son, born of a woman, born subject to [the regulations of] the Law, To purchase the freedom of (to ransom, to redeem, to atone for) those who were subject to the Law, that we might be adopted and have Sonship conferred upon us [and be recognized as God's sons]."

You see Jesus, being the Door, has purchased our freedom from the law and this has opened a new Door that brings us into His grace.

The function and assignment of a Door is twofold. It acts as a barrier or a protector to prevent disasters. As well as, it brings us into divine revelation and understanding which sets us free from all that tries to entangle us.

How are we liberators and doors?

As children of God, we too are called to open the Door of Christ to others. We open a Door to others as we plant seeds of love in their lives. To do this is to give people the opportunity to experience God in a practical way.

The Lord will use us to bring liberty to people as we seek Him prophetically to expose barriers that have caused people to be in bondage. So often in our lives and many others, we see the same wandering that we see in Exodus as the people of Israel took forty years to do an eleven day journey. If we look at the root of what caused the Israelites journey to be prolonged, we will see that it was complaining and having a poor attitude. So often we are going through a wilderness season and God will send someone with the keys to open the door of your promised land. However, if we fail to recognise the key, or choose not to adhere to the guidance given we could find ourselves aimlessly wandering for a long time.

Refuse to be a stumbling block to others

As Children of God we need to be mindful that we are doors or gateways into the Kingdom of Heaven. When we understand the privilege of this, by God's grace, we will ensure that we are not stumbling blocks to anyone either. The Bible says in Matthew 23:13;

> *"But woe to you, scribes and Pharisees, pretenders (hypocrites)! For your shut the kingdom of heaven in men faces; for you neither enter yourselves, nor do you allow those who are about to go in to do so."*

As doors or gateways, we have an important responsibility to rest in the finished work of Christ and drink from the Holy Spirit the enablement to lead people in the paths of righteousness for His name's sake.

How to identify a door?

It must also be noted that a door is an access point or entry point and there are many varieties of access. We can gain access through any of our gateways; eyes, ears, nostrils, mouth, hands, feet, etc. Scripture highlights that when a door was shown in scripture, spiritual senses were used. Chronicles 9:6;

> ***Nevertheless I did not believe their reports until I came and my eyes had seen it. And behold, the half of the greatness of your wisdom was not told me. You surpass the report that I heard.***

Again in Job 13:1;

Seeing yourself through the eyes of Jesus

"Behold, my eye has seen all this, my ear has heard and understood it."

And in Matthew 13:17;

For truly I say to you that many prophets and righteous men desired to see what you see, and did not see it, and to hear what you hear, and did not hear it.

So, seeing and hearing in the spiritual realm are criteria for the supernatural doors or gateways to be accessed. Numerous times in scripture I have read where Jesus has trans-located from one place to another. Luke 4:28:30 describes the crowd as enraged; **they got up and drove Him out of the city, and led Him to the brow of the Hill... in order to throw him off the cliff. But passing through their midst, He went His way."** Jesus literally walked through the people. Why? Because

He is the door. Again, when Jesus stepped in the boat with His disciples (John 6:21), ***"they were willing to receive Him into the boat and immediately the boat was at the land to which they were going."*** The word "immediately" is the operative word here; implying that they were supernaturally accelerated to their destination.

Another renowned passage used for translocation is in Acts 8:39-40, ***"when they came up out of the water, the Spirit of the Lord snatched Philip away. And the Eunuch no longer saw him....but Phillip found Himself in Azotus"*** some distance away. It is believed that Azotus where Phillip found himself was 270 furlongs from his original destination Gaza. One could say, the Holy Spirit ushered Phillip through a supernatural door by translocation.

Seeing yourself through the eyes of Jesus

So you see, biblically we can go through the Door of Jesus and translocate just like these examples. I myself have bi-located (being two places at once) numerous times. Saying that should not alarm you, because the Bible already tells us that "we are seated in heavenly places", implying that as spirit beings living in a body, we are living in a bi-located state all the time. We are in Heaven but we are on Earth.

Psalm 37:4 says that God grants us the desires of our heart. Recently I have had such a burden in my heart for the Jews in Iraq who have been persecuted by the Muslim extremists. I so desire for the Lord to sovereignly trans-locate me to Iraq to care for and to free others from any form of oppression. I am yet to trans-locate, but in the same way I prayed for a year for my spiritual eyes to open and another year for my spiritual ears to open, my prayer is "Daddy God I thank you that my body and soul are one with my spirit and like

Jesus, Peter, and the Saints of old were translocated, I too ask for You to move me supernaturally so that I can be of help to the Jewish people. Use me to convert Muslims in Jesus' name, amen.

Declaration

Jesus thank You for being the DOOR to our freedom. I declare a freedom to walk in Your truth. A freedom to rest in Your pastures not trying to earn through works. Thank You that as Your child I carry keys to this door so I can invite others to walk in this awesome freedom. I declare freedom to choose to enter into Your awesome presence and be transformed by the renewing of my mind. I declare freedom to choose Your ways and not my ways; freedom to eat the good of the land because of my obedience and willingness. Freedom to translocate from one place to another as the Holy Spirit leads.

Day 4:

Jesus – A Child

> *"Out of the mouth of Babes and unweaned infants You have established strength because of Your foes, that You might silence the enemy and the avenger." (Psalm 8:2, Amp)*

The Bible says that out of the mouth of babes, the enemy would be silenced. This speaks volumes about the power a child has because of their purity and simplicity of heart. There is power in purity; simplicity induces our faith. When things are complicated in times of application, we are more likely to be doubtful because the information becomes muddled.

Although I am in my 40's, when I speak to my Mom or Dad I see myself as their child. There are some expectations, as a daughter, I have of them because they are my parents. Interestingly, in all my encounters with God I have always seen myself as a child. No matter how old we are in the natural we are still a child of our parents. Jesus himself encourages us to be like little children. He does not mean to be childish, but to be childlike. There are some qualities that children have that makes them so endearing. They are fearless, they are pure hearted, they are free, not guarded, and they are simple, not complicated. You see, already there are so many qualities that can be emulated.

At 12 years old Jesus was perceived in so many amazing ways. Luke 2:40-52 describes Jesus as a child:
- He grew both spiritually and physically (v40)
- He was filled with and grew in wisdom (v40, v52)

- God's favour rested upon Him (v40)
- He had exceptional understanding of the scriptures (v47)
- He illustrated a profound teaching gift (v47)
- He knew His life's mission (v49)
- He subjected Himself under His parents authority (v51)
- He grew in favour with God and man (v52)

Jesus knew His mission

In verse 49, Jesus inquired of His parents;

> *"How is it that you sought after me? Did you not know I am suppose to be about my Father's business?"*

My understanding of His questions, reveals to us the depth of His convictions, even at 12 years old, of His mission/assignment. Jesus was amazed that they would be looking for Him aimlessly. I believe Jesus was alarmed at their unbelief because of the supernatural revelations Mary and Joseph were privy to. Jesus implied these revelations were clues of where He would be; the house of the Lord.

I believe like Jesus, in our gut we have a sense of what we will be, but throughout our lives we are given important clues that are essential to our calling. There are some things we are drawn to, passionate about, dream about and long for. Your parents may be oblivious to your mission, but from a child we have a sense of purpose. From the time we were conceived those things that are unique to our make-up were deposited; we are born knowing. As we grow up, we must not begin to doubt and reason away what we already know in our hearts. Clearly, from Jesus' example, it is for the child to demonstrate who they are and in response, the parents guide and nurture accordingly. This is why the Bible says to train up a child according to their individual bent. Your mission is already innately built in; it will naturally come out. Jesus knew who He was and He determined where He would be or go; so it is with us.

Do you know your mission? Your mission is entwined with your passions. Ask yourself what would you do without being paid?

He grew in favour with God and man
Knowing our identity provides a strong basis for our lives and how well we will function on this Earth. Jesus grew in favour with God and man because He remained true to who God said He was and would be. He was not dissuaded by societal norms and practices. He knew who He was. He embraced Himself. He was driven by His identity in His Father in Heaven. Whose identity are you driven by?

Experience has taught me that, if you have a strong sense of your real identity, you carry a strong presence of God and as a result people are drawn to you because you exude such peace. Please note it is favour with God that draws people. This immediately eliminates the need to seek the approval of men. Life has taught me that you can only give what you have. Therefore confidence will always birth confidence, not fear. I believe therefore, when people see someone who is comfortable in their own skin, if they are not, they will be drawn to you, hoping to bring forth that in themselves - this is favour with man. This favour comes when you have already established being under His authority, releasing you to be a child who carries God's favour.

Jesus also found out His gifts from earlier on and He exercised them. He was a good teacher; Jesus embraced His gifts and flowed in them. The Bible says in Proverbs 18:16 that our gifts will make room for us. This tells me that when we use our gifts, we invite God's favour and the favour from man into our lives. Every gift we have enables us to meet the needs of others. Like any other gift, the more we use it, the more we grow in wisdom and are able to direct people on how to develop their own gift. The Bible says in Hebrews 5:14;

"Solid food are for those whose senses have been trained by practice so as to distinguish between what is morally good and what is evil."

So we see that it is by practise that we not only develop our gifts, but we are able to sharpen them and also help others in developing their gifts too.

Declaration

As He is so am I. Therefore, I confess that no matter how old I am, I am a child of God. I confess with my mouth that like any child I will look to the Father as my Source. I am a child of God, my identity is rooted in Jesus the Word who became flesh. I choose to embrace who I am in Him fully. I am pure in heart, I am conscious of God, I am simple. I embrace all that God the Father has deposited in me and set my heart to use it for His glory and to bless others. I declare that as Jesus fulfilled His destiny, I too will fulfil my destiny and I will have favour with God and man, and walk in godly wisdom.

Day 5:

Jesus – Son of God

> *"Now I say that the heir, as long as he is a child, does not differ at all from a slave, though he is master of all, but is under guardians and stewards until the time appointed by the father"* (Galatians 4:1-2, NKJV)

This scripture highlights to us that being an heir to a promise does not mean you will automatically inherit the promise. We all have to go through a process. As an earthly parent, if I have a business and my sons have not showed themselves to be responsible or good stewards through training, though by right they are heirs, I would not give them the responsibility until they are ready. For two reasons:-

1. To show myself as a responsible steward before God.
2. To protect my sons from failure.

When Jesus was baptised in water, the Father spoke over Him and said; **"This is my beloved Son, in whom I am well pleased"** (Matthew 3:17). You see, the Father tells us who we are first, then tells us to go and live it out. I believe God the Father was declaring or prophesying over Jesus His desired relationship with His Son. It is important to note; this was when Jesus was about to step out into His divine calling.

Conversely in Matthew 17:5, we see Jesus with His disciples upon the Mount of Tabor where He was transfigured. The Father said; **"This is my beloved son in whom I am well pleased. Hear Him!"** If you look at both statements you will see there is a distinct difference; one statement was prophetic or a statement of potential, while the other was a statement of maturity. God the Father added to this statement "HEAR HIM!" which implies a new level of authority worthy for others to listen to Him. When we are trained or equipped we can attain a place of maturity, He then releases us to be sons of God.

Characteristics of a son of God

In Galatians 4:4-7 it says;

> ***"But when the fullness of the time came God sent forth His Son, born of a woman under the law, so that He may redeem those under the law, that we may receive the adoption of sons. Because you are sons, God has sent forth the Spirit of His Son into our hearts and we cry out "Abba! Father! Therefore you are no longer a slave but a son and if a son therefore an heir through God."***

This scripture clearly outlines the characteristics of a son. A son:-
1. Redeems those that are under the law.
2. is no longer a slave
3. is a heir through God

"For you have not received a spirit of slavery leading to fear again but you have received a spirit of adoption by which we cry out Abba Father! The Spirit Himself testifies that we are children of God, and if children heirs also heirs of God and fellow heirs of Christ, if indeed we suffer with Him so we may also be glorified with Him. For I consider that the sufferings of this present time are not worthy to be compared with the glory that is revealed to us. For the anxious longing of creation waits eagerly for the revealing of the sons of God."

Romans 8:15-19 reiterates the characteristics of Sonship and adds: -

4. A son has gone through the process of dying with Christ so they can be glorified with Him.
5. A son carries the Spirit of adoption not an orphan spirit.

Characteristics of a son of God

Sons are led by the spirit of God *Romans 8:14*	Sons are devoted to knowing Christ intimately
Sons are not under the law *Galatians 4:5*	Sons model the life of Ascension or glorification; they are one with Christ in His death
Sons have learned the benefits of submission and being under legitimate authority	Sons understand the importance of freedom in Christ and seek to liberate others *Galatians 4:4*
Sons understand that authority flows from love not control	Sons care about their Father's business rather than their own *John 5:19*
Sons carry the central ministry of Jesus	Sons are heirs partaking of their full inheritance

We must also note that sons of God are led by the Spirt of God, not by their five natural senses. Isaiah 43:19 says; ***"See, I am doing a new thing! Now it springs up; do you not perceive it?"*** We cannot use our natural mind to figure out spiritual things; we need to perceive. Isaiah also prophesied in the 11th chapter that Jesus would not judge by His eyes nor His ears. The empowering and the equipping we receive to perceive is not based on our physical senses but according to our spiritual senses. That is, what we are drawn to, have a gut feeling of or an impression of; it is bottom line Spirit led.

How are we trained to be sons?

Speaking prophetically about Jesus Isaiah 11:1-3 says;

> ***"Then a shoot will spring from the stem of Jesse, and a branch from its roots will bear fruit. The Spirit of the Lord will***

rest on Him. The spirit of wisdom and understanding. The spirit of counsel and strength, The spirit of knowledge and fear of the Lord. "

The chapter begins, by highlighting to its readers whom this prophecy is for, by reminding us of the lineage Jesus came through. It then describes the seven spirits that would be on Jesus. These seven spirits would each play a specific role to empower Jesus to walk or to live out the results described in the rest of the passage.

"He will delight in the fear of the Lord, He will not judge by what is eyes see, nor make a decision by what His ears hear but with righteousness He will judge the poor; and decide with fairness for the afflicted of the earth; And He will strike the earth with the rod of His mouth, And with the breath

of His lips He will He will slay the wicked. Also righteousness will be the belt of His loins and faithfulness the belt about His waist."

Interestingly, from the seven spirits listed, the spirit of the fear of the Lord is highlighted as the one Jesus delighted in because it enabled Him to judge correctly, fairly and to walk in righteousness. We are often baffled by how it was that Jesus never sinned; this scripture highlights the value Jesus placed on the Spirit of the Fear of the Lord; when you do, you will not sin. 1 John 5:18 reiterates this and says;

"We know that no one who is born of God sins; but He who was born of God keeps him, and evil one does not touch Him."

Living a sinless life is attainable because the Spirit of the Fear of the Lord is what enables us. This does not mean to be afraid, but to be in awe, captivated, enthralled and in wonder of God Himself. This spirit brings us into alignment through accountability.

A few years ago when I found out about these 7 spirits and began to understand their functions, I was drawn to the Spirit of Wisdom. In fact, after much studying, I told the Lord in patois (broken English) "dis one I want" (translation: I want this one). That afternoon as I napped, I had a dream that was more like a vision. It was overwhelmingly REAL. I saw my husband and I in our bedroom getting dressed. My husband quickly went to the door to look out, as if he had heard a sound and turned and remarked, "someone is coming." I then said with annoyance, "tell them they can't come we are getting dressed." As I said this he looked again and backed away from the door in fear and said, "They are coming"... He quivered.

I was now even more annoyed when the door flew open and as it did, a bright light shone into the room. The light was blinding and captivating at the same time. As I peered closely, there was a woman standing there in a skirt suit. I was not sure if she wore a silver suit or a white suit because of the brilliance of the light. I put my right hand up impulsively to stop whomever it was from coming in, but I was brought to a halt when I realised this was not a human being. As I stared at her in unbelief, I heard an audible voice speak from within me and boomed, "This is the Spirit of Wisdom!" As I heard the voice instinctively the Spirit of wisdom smiled as if she too had heard the same voice and then I fell in the spirit as if I were dead.

Seeing yourself through the eyes of Jesus

When I awoke that afternoon, I was completely in AWE because my room was filled with the awesome presence of God. I could hardly speak. Proverbs 4:5-9 refers to the Spirit of Wisdom as a female. Also in Revelations 4:5 it describes these seven spirits as being around the throne of God which would explain the magnificent heavenly atmosphere that engulfed my room. Suffice to say, after that visit our family saw more money than we have ever seen before. I began to see a new level of manifestation of the gifts of the Spirit in operation in me. She not only visited, but by her visit she demonstrated her function that she equips us for position and prosperity. She teaches us how to judge and how to bring justice. She releases contentment and joy to you and those around you.

Solomon is a great example of someone who was endowed with the Spirit of Wisdom. As outlined, each spirit has a specific function. For us to be trained by them we (like Jesus) must value or take delight in them and the role they want to play in our lives to equip us for HIS Glory.

Functions of the seven spirits

Spirit of the Lord	Mandates us for position *Isaiah 61:1*
Spirit of Wisdom	Equips us for position *Ephesians 1:17*
Spirit of Understanding	Authorises us for position *Colossians 1:9*
Spirit of Counsel	Prepares us for position *Psalm 1:1*
Spirit of Knowledge	Empowers us for position *1 Corinthians 2:1-5*
Spirit of Might	Reveals us for Position *2 Corinthians 10: 4*
Spirit of the Fear of the Lord	Brings us into accountability for position *2 Timothy 1:7*

What do we look like when we become sons in the spiritual realm?

Jesus had not only grasped how to operate and function in the attributes of the seven spirits; He also learned how to reveal the characteristic traits hence why He was transfigured on the mountain.

We need to look at what it looks like to be transfigured if we are really going to understand what it looks like when one becomes a son. The word transfigured in the Greek is 'metamorphoo', meaning a change in appearance. This is an outward change, an unveiling of the inner glory that is veiled in flesh. Jesus became to His disciples, the visible manifestation of God's presence. The description of Jesus on the mount is similar to what is described in Hebrews 1:3; ***"The Son is the radiance of God's glory the exact representation of His being."*** When we give our lives to Christ an inner change occurs, but when we become sons of God, an outer change occurs in that the inner life of Christ begins to show onto the physical parts. When we are transfigured, the change in us is a complete transformation; inside and out. As described in the scripture above we become the radiance of God's glory.

In Revelations, Apostle John described the full manifestation of the Son of Man (JESUS) who had been mentored by the seven spirits. In Revelation 1:15-16 it reads;

> **"His feet glowed like burnished (bright) bronze as it is refined in a furnace, and His voice was like the sound of many waters. In His right hand He held seven stars, and from His mouth there came forth a sharp two edged sword, and His face was like the sun shining in full power at midday."**

Remember **"as Jesus is so are we in this world."** If it happened to Jesus, surely it will happen to us. The first time I experience this I was worshipping in song passionately when I began to burn with the FIRE of God. My prayer that day was "let no one see me; only Jesus." As I was singing, I became aware that I became invisible, transparent or translucent on one side of my body. Another time I was in a meeting, the leader called me out and prayed for my hands because she saw my hands lit up. The prophet Isaiah in chapter 60 prophesied that this would happen from verses 1-3 In the latter part of verse 2-3 he said "the Lord will arise over you and the glory of the will be seen upon you. So you see, as Jesus is so are we in this world.

Let's go a bit deeper now... The other thing noted here is that Jesus was able to communicate with the cloud of witnesses; in this case it was Elijah and Moses. I believe Sonship is a place in

Christ that allows us to speak with the cloud of witnesses. Matthew 17:2-3;

> **"There He was transfigured before them. His face shone like the sun, and His clothes became as white as the light. Just then there appeared before them Moses and Elijah, talking with Jesus."**

I have not personally had a conversation with the cloud of witness (Saints of old). Although I have definitely witnessed the cloud of witnesses, I was so in awe, taking to them was the furthest from my mind. This is a great lesson to learn... when the cloud of witnesses show up, don't just stare in awe; engage, by asking questions. Jesus spoke to them. As you can see, we have a limitless scope of inheritance available to us as sons of God. I encourage you, to begin to submit yourselves to be trained and mentored by the seven Spirits as

God transforms you forever. Begin by inviting one of the seven Spirits to train you. Study that spirit out biblically and apply accordingly.

Declaration

Father I declare that as Jesus is so am I. Therefore, I declare that I will wilfully submit to the seven Spirits that Jesus Himself submitted to, so that I can walk in full Son-ship. I declare like Jesus was transfigured and shone with Your glory that I too, by my willingness to be taught and trained, will shine from the inside out and many will see Jesus instead of me. I declare that I too will be able to communicate with the cloud of witnesses as Jesus did. I declare Father be glorified through me in Jesus name.

Day 6:

Jesus – King of Kings

> *Jesus said "All authority has been given to me in heaven and on earth"* (Matthew 28:18b)

Jesus Himself has acknowledged that He has all authority. If Jesus has all authority then we too have this authority because (2 Corinthians 5:20) says that **"we are ambassadors for Christ, as though God were pleading through us;"** As we walk in oneness through being reconciled to God we are His representatives. We have the same authority as Jesus. He would not call us to partner with Him and leave us helpless nor powerless.

A kingly anointing is a governmental anointing that brings the world systems in alignment with Heaven's economy. As we activate our kingly anointing we can synchronise Heaven with Earth. We pray and declare as Jesus taught us (Luke 11:1-4) **"as it is in heaven so it must be on earth."** This anointing enables you to walk in the power and authority necessary to declare **"decree a thing and it will be established for you"(Job 22:28)**. This authority equips us to walk in divine dominion.

The word *authority* can be perceived as a very controversial word. Too often in life we experience people who had positions of authority but they used their position to trample, to abuse and in so many cases damage people's confidence and self-esteem. When you have been the recipient of this bad treatment, it can create a desire and a justification to be rebellious. However, I have learnt that this is satan's way to steal the blessings which come from being under authority. What we have failed to realise is that to embrace God's given authority with the right heart is to open the doors for God to give greater authority. In Matthew 8:5-10 the Bible tells of a centurion who came to beseech Jesus' help to heal his servant. As he observed the miracles Jesus performed something became apparent to him. The Bible describes this in verse 9-10....

> ***"For I also am a man under authority, having soldiers under me. And I say to this one, Go, and he goes; and to another, Come, and he comes; and to my slave, Do this, and he does it."***

I have read this passage numerous times but I missed the significance of those two words *"I also."* As I inquired of the Lord what it meant, I realised the Centurion recognised the authority Jesus had and he accredited it to the fact that He

(Jesus) was a man under authority. He recognised that the same authority he himself used to say to his servant go and he goes is the same authority Jesus was using with sickness. Jesus has the amazing ability to command a thing and see it happen. The Centurion knew that Jesus was under a higher power for Him to speak the word of healing and his servant would be healed. As he witnessed the amazing miracles that Jesus performed he recognised the power that comes from being under authority. Whose authority are you under?

From the beginning God gave us tremendous authority. He told Adam that he had dominion over the entire Earth. Due to their disobedience and failure to come under God's authority they instead came under satan's authority and lost their God given authority. Today because of Jesus' sacrifice on the cross we can take back the authority we gave to Satan by coming under God's authority.

Failing to come under the Lord's authority is to give authority to satan over our lives. What authority do we possess? Jesus tells us in Luke 10:19;

> *"He has given us authority to tread upon serpents and scorpions and over all the power of the enemy, and nothing by any means hurt us."*

In John 14:12 Jesus said;

> *"Truly Truly, I say to you, he who believes in Me, the works that I do, he will do also, and greater works than these He will do; because I go to the Father."*

In John 5: 19;

> *"The Son of Man can do nothing from Himself except what He sees the Father*

doing, for whatever that One does, these things the Son also does in like manner."

Jesus was committed to pleasing and honouring the Father. Jesus' knew that the Father was His authority. As a result, He did nothing in His own strength. He had nothing to prove so he had no need to dabble in seeking the approval of men, nor selfish ambition. As Jesus submitted to the authority of the Father we must submit to the Lordship of Jesus in our lives. May we also say "I can do all things through Christ who gives me strength. I can do nothing of myself except what I see Jesus do, for whatever He does I too can do and will do in the same manner and greater will He do through me."

Is Jesus your authority? If not, make a decision now to come under His authority in all areas of your life.

Now that we know how to walk in authority, what are our symbols of this authority? A king wears a crown, a robe, has a sceptre in the hand and sits on the throne. The Bible already says that Christ **"raised us with Him and seated us with Him in heavenly places in Jesus."** (Ephesians 2:6) we have a throne in Heaven.

Crowns

As believers we have a crown/crowns and the Bible is clear about these crowns. A crown is a symbol that is recognised in the spirit world. In Acts 19:15 it says **"....and the evil spirit answered and said "Jesus I know, and Paul I know but who are you?"** Here is an example, where the evil spirits themselves did not recognize the authority (crown) of these believers. Though they were saying the right words, they had no authority. I believe these believers were seen as parrots or a crown of mockery in the spirit. They were simply repeating what they saw and heard but had no personal conviction of their own. They were unaware of their own spiritual state and so the evil spirits mocked and jeered them.

A crown is symbolic of the representative of a realm of government. A king cannot be represented without a crown. The ability to see in the spiritual realm like Jesus is a privilege because we are able to see people as Jesus sees them. I often say that when I turn in my bed the enemy and his cohorts are trembling in their boots because they know what I carry. You see a crown mandates us to fulfil a purpose. I thought I was just a kitten until one day I asked the Lord how He sees me and I heard "A LION". I thought I was hearing wrong so I asked Him to confirm...when in an instant someone took the microphone and sang a song that was calling for the lions to come out. When we are being who we truly are, the enemy has to run. If I am being a dog when I am cat, then I will not be able to use the authority that

Seeing yourself through the eyes of Jesus

comes with being cat. I encourage you to ask the Lord, how He sees you.

Jesus spoke to the Pharisees as they were represented in the spirit; "hypocrites! Whitewashed tombs...full of dead men's bones and all uncleanness...brood of vipers (Matthew 23:27-28). Here the Lord Jesus saw the crown the Pharisees wore which is the crown of death.

So you see, crowns are signs we are recognised by. Let us look at different examples of crowns the Bible outlines and what they represent. As you do, ask the Holy Spirit to highlight any you have so that you can be aware of your true identity in the spirit. Also, as you look, begin to ask the Father to release ones you know you don't have.

Name of Crowns	Scripture Reference	Purpose of the crown	Information on crowns
Crown of righteousness	2 Timothy 4:8 Finally, there is laid up for me the crown of righteousness, which the Lord, the righteous judge, will give to me on that Day, and not to me only but also to all who loved His appearing."	Received at salvation in order to live out righteousness	This crown is given to those who love His appearing You can lose this crown when we repeatedly wilfully sin. Failing to acknowledge and use this crown can result in repetitive sin.
Crown of life	James 1:12 Blessed is the man who endures temptation, for when he has been approved, he will receive the Crown of life which the Lord has promised to those who love Him.	Received through the trials of life and our dealings with temptations when we overcome.	When you receive this crown it releases the life of God in your life; with the ability to stand on His promises concerning you; hence the ability to overcome.

Seeing yourself through the eyes of Jesus

Name of crowns	Scripture Reference	Purpose of the Crown	Information on crowns
Crown of Glory	1 Peter 5:4 "when the Chief Shepherd appears, you will receive the Crown of Glory that does not fade away"	When you begin to live out Christ revealing Him everywhere you go, then, you are a king and the glory of God manifest.	The crown of Glory manifest the supernatural realm on Earth. This crown is for those who not only speak the Word but live the Word.
Crown of the Anointing Oil	Leviticus 21:12 Neither shall he go out of the anointing oil of his God is upon him.	Received where we Have encountered the Presence of God in a deeply relational way.	When you express this relationship by bringing the Kingdom to Earth this crown is Manifested. The anointing oil burns demons causing them to flee.
Incorruptible Crown	1 Corinthians 9:25 "And every man that strives for self-control is temperate in all things, Now they do it to obtain a corruptible crown; but we an incorruptible"	This crown is manifested due to our surrender to God, obeying Him and pursuing His Presence.	We are made clean in His Presence and so His presence keeps us incorruptible. This crown is given to those who have disciplined their bodies.

Names of crowns	Scripture Reference	Purpose of the Crown	Information on crowns
Crown of Rejoicing	1 Thessalonians 2:19 For what is our hope, or joy, or crown of rejoicing?'	This crown brings an overflow of joy that will make unbelievers think you are drunk like the apostles in the book of Acts - even though it was 9:00 in the morning.	Joy of the Lord is your strength Nehemiah 8:10. This crown is manifested by your daily unbroken fellowship with God. This crown is associated with soul winners.
Crown of Separation/ Holiness	Numbers 6:8; 1 Peter 2:9-10 But you are a chosen generation, a royal priesthood, an holy nation, a peculiar people; that you should show forth the praises of Him who has called you out of darkness into his marvellous light;	This crown separates us from the world and sets us apart to be holy.	We are consecrated to God for His sacred use. We are priest, kings unto our GOD. People see us and no we are different. Children and animals are drawn to you because of the separation that is evident.

There are crowns that are considered bad, like the crown of pride, crown of thorns and the crown of corruptible. I would love to mention briefly the crown of thorns and its significance. The Crown of thorns was woven together when Jesus was being ridiculed and mocked on the cross. However, when we look at the word "thorn" when it was first mentioned, it was when Adam sinned and released the curse of sin on mankind. Genesis 3:17-18;

> **And to Adam He said, "Because you have listened to the voice of your wife and have eaten of the tree of which I commanded you, 'You shall not eat of it,' cursed is the ground because of you; in pain you shall eat of it all the days of your life; thorns and thistles it shall bring forth for you; and you shall eat the plants of the field.**

This scripture shows us that sin had indirectly and directly produced for us a crown of thorns. By

Jesus being spitefully adorned with this same crown, He not only identified with us in our sin, but also nullified any need for us to adorn ourselves with a crown of thorns because of His redemptive sacrifice. Jesus took the crown of thorns, but now He has been crowned with glory and honour. Hebrews 2:9 says;

> ***"But we see Him who for a little while was made lower than the angels, namely Jesus, crowned with glory and honour because of the suffering of death, so that by the grace of God He might taste death for everyone."***

Like Jesus, let's choose to divinely exchange the crown of thorns (sin) for the crown of glory and honour. In the same way, we can lose a bad crown for a good crown; so too we can lose a good crown. How would we know if we have lost a crown? The things you were able to do you can no

Seeing yourself through the eyes of Jesus

longer do. The grace you once had to read your Bible for hours on end is no longer there. The sensitivity you once had for spiritual things is gone. If you have recognised that you have lost your crown, you can have it back. You only need to repent of whatever you have allowed to steal it or renounce any ungodly vows you made. In Revelations 3:11 Jesus encourages us; ***"I am coming soon. Hold on to what you have, so that no one will take your crown."***

1. Identify with the help of the Holy Spirit when you lost it (you may find it was during a difficult circumstance that you made a vow that cost you your crown; or wounds that you never dealt with.
2. Confess your sins to PAPA God and ask Him to show you His perspective on the matter. As He does, it will bring healing, revelation and direction.

3. By faith reclaim your crown and wear it with honour.

A Sceptre

A sceptre is a symbol of royal power and authority. The word sceptre is most times referred to as the rod or a staff. It is seen as a tool to rule. In the Old Testament the Bible prophesies that Jesus is a sceptre. Genesis 49:8-12;

> *"Judah, you are he whom your brothers shall praise; Your hand shall be on the neck of your enemies; Your father's children shall bow down before you. Judah is a lion's whelp; from the prey, my son, you have gone up. He bows down, he lies down as a lion; and as a lion, who shall rouse him? The SCEPTRE shall not depart from Judah, Nor a lawgiver from between his feet until Shiloh comes; And to Him shall be the*

obedience of the people. Binding his donkey to the vine and his donkey's colt to the choice vine, He washed his garments in wine and his clothes in the blood of grapes. His eyes are darker than wine and his teeth whiter than milk."

In the New Testament, Jesus said that all power and authority has been given to Him (Matthew 28:18-20) as a result of His finished work (*"it is finished"*). We are given a sceptre to appropriate the finished work of Christ on the Earth. How are you doing with that? Every-time we choose to claim our inheritance that was bought by Jesus' blood we are using our sceptre. This could be healing, prosperity, love, peace, glory, grace, acceptance etc.

A Ring

Do you have a ring? A king wears a ring. We see this in Luke 15, when the prodigal son return, a ring was placed on his finger. A ring in marriage usually signifies a marriage without end or an eternal covenant. A reminder of the covenant we made with the King of kings.

Ancient kings used signet rings to designate authority, honour, or ownership. Zerubbabel can be seen as a typology of Jesus because in Haggai 2:23, Zerubbabel was called the Lord's signet ring; Zerubbabel built the temple. In the New Testament we see Jesus Christ, who will establish His people in the Promised Land, construct an even grandeur temple, one that will last forever. If as He is so are we, we must therefore see our temple as a place of never-ending worship, in spirit and truth to our God.

A Mantle

Where is your Mantle? In Bible times, a mantle was an outer cloak used for additional covering and warmth, especially at night. The mantle was essentially the only "blanket" the person had, so even when used as a pledge the law required it be returned before bedtime. Elijah wore a mantle that was given to Elisha. Jesus wore a mantle and He promised we would do greater works than He did (John 14:12).

The anointing that was on Jesus' mantle is available to every believer to be His greater works. To carry this mantle Jesus gave us is be under His covering; if we don't, we are leaving our backs exposed to the enemy (1 Kings 19:13). By faith put on that mantle and wear it; make yourself available for Him to use you as His greater works.

Christine Nelson

Declaration

My Father is the King of kings. He (King) has authority over me I am that lower case king. I am under His authority and as I submit to His authority doing what I am told, I walk in greater authority. I am a princess/prince therefore how I speak, my attire and conduct reflects my royal status. I am a person of influence, I am born to rule and to reign. I have been given authority to trample on serpents, to decree and declare a thing and it will come to pass, because I am under authority. As a king I declare that I am submissive to the KING of KINGS He rules over my tongue. So that the power of my tongue will carry HIS Power. I declare that as a king I will not just have crowns, but I wear my crowns with power and authority. I declare that I will never have my back uncovered but I will live out the mantle that has been placed on me. I am indeed Jesus' Greater works and His mantle will remind me that He is my covering. I will be His signet ring reminding me of the oneness I share with Him for eternity. I declare that I will use my sceptre to apply Your finished work. I will continue to rule with my sceptre until I see the full manifestation of all that has been purchased for me on the cross - in my life and the life of others.

Day 7:

Jesus – Bread of Life

> *Jesus said to them, "I am the bread of life; he who comes to Me will not hunger, and he who believes in Me will never thirst. (John 6:35)*

I love this scripture, I have purposed to believe it and to live it. I believe because I go to Jesus when I am hungry physically, spiritually, emotionally and psychologically, I will NEVER hunger. I believe He will quench my thirst, so that, I will NOT be parched. Do you see Jesus as your food and your drink?

What does Jesus mean by being the bread of life?

The term Bread of Life can be perceived as bread which upon consumption brings life. Jesus answered this question in verse 50-51 in the same chapter;

> **_"This is the bread which comes down out of heaven, so that one may eat of it and not die. I am the living bread that came down out of heaven; if anyone eats of this bread, he will live forever; and the bread also which I will give for the life of the world is My flesh."_**

Jesus spoke of Himself as the Living Bread and as an eternal Bread. A living bread is Bread that is alive, which suggest to me, when eaten, it has the ability to configure, align, attune or create change. This Bread of Life is also eternal, when consumed you cannot die. To consume the Lord is to take Him into ourselves for Him to be One with our spirit man. Jesus wants to be the life giving Bread in our lives so we can be like Him in word and deed.

A desire to do good works is good, but the motivation needs to be of God. Lucifer (Isaiah 14:12-14) and Adam (Genesis 3:1-14) both had a noble desire to be like God but the motive behind their desire and the methods they used were motivated by rebellion. We should desire the Bread of Life more than food, but we must go about it by following the example of Christ who emptied Himself taking the form of a servant unto death. (Philippians 2:5-11).

In John 6:26 Jesus said;

> ***"Verily verily, I say unto you,"Ye seek me not because ye saw the miracles, but because ye did eat of the loaves,***

and were filled. Labour not for the meat which perishes but for that meat which endures unto everlasting life, which the son of man shall give unto you for him hath God the Father sealed."

Jesus warns us not to seek perishable food but to seek Him who is our life supply, the only food that will sustain and give eternal life. It brings me back to the distinction that I made between the tree of life and the tree of the knowledge of good and evil in my second book "Transformed by Oneness into His likeness".

Jesus is the tree of life. He is all we need to live fulfilled lives. The tree of knowledge brings death which involves the five natural senses. The tree of life on the other hand, brings life. I believe the tree of life represents that incorruptible seed that 1 Peter 1:23 talks about;

"Being born again, not of corruptible seed, but of incorruptible, by the word of God, which lives and abides for ever."

You see when we eat of the wrong tree it kills us spiritually. When we eat of the BREAD of LIFE, the TREE OF LIFE, THE INCORRUPTIBLE SEED, we awaken our spiritual senses and begin to perceive the things of God and nourish the spirit being that we are.

As believers we talk a lot more about Jesus' redemption rather than Jesus being our food. In the Ark of the Covenant there were three objects which represented Jesus Christ – the **Manna**, **Aaron's rod** and **Tablets of stone**. Hebrews 9:3-4;

> "***Behind the second veil there was a tabernacle which is called the Holy of***

Holies, having a golden altar of incense and the ark of the covenant covered on all sides with gold, in which was a golden jar holding the manna, and Aaron's rod which budded, and the tables of the covenant. "

I would like to expand on the manna which was the Israelites only source of food and contained all the nutrients needed to sustain them on their journey. It was God's perfect food for them then, today God's perfect food for us is Jesus the Bread of life. He is the one that will strengthen us, sustain us on our journey. It was Jesus who said;

"Truly truly, I say to you, it is not Moses who has given you the bread out of Heaven, but it is My Father who gives you the true Bread out of heaven. For the Bread of God is that which comes down out of heaven, and gives life to

the world....I am the Bread of Life; he who comes to Me will not hunger, and he who believes in Me will never thirst." (John 6:32-35).

I was challenged by a young man who boldly proclaimed, he no longer ate because of fear that he might become weak, or ate because he was fearful he would have a headache, but purely because of pleasure. Instead he focused on communing with the Bread of life as his food and he knew that it was able to prevent a headache, sickness, diseases or any kind of weakness. As he shared, I was brought back to the origin of the Israelites consuming the manna and indeed it sustained them.

Today, is no different we only need to repent of their idolatry or religion of food, we have come to believe. Which outlines we must eat breakfast, lunch and dinner and a snack in between.

We have conditioned our natural mind with that belief while Jesus says; **"I am the Bread of Life; he who comes to me will not hunger."** What if the natural food is symbolic to the Tree of the knowledge of good and evil and the Tree of Life is symbolic of Jesus Himself? Are we not therefore looking to the wrong tree to sustain us? AGAIN? I have endeavoured to ask the Lord to change my mind-set towards food; to see Jesus as my food, the one that sustains. I do eat natural food, to eat that for pleasure and not out fear or greed. In Matthew 4:4 "Jesus said;

"It is written, 'MAN SHALL NOT LIVE ON BREAD ALONE, BUT ON EVERY WORD THAT PROCEEDS OUT OF THE MOUTH OF GOD."

*Please note I am not encouraging nor advocating people not to eat, but to change the mind-set of why we eat food.

How do we consume the Bread of Life?

- By reading, meditating
- Speaking His Word
- Living His Word
- Communion
- Singing His Word
- Praying His word (John 6:54)

From the list above I would like to elaborate on Communion, Meditation and Living His Word as one.

Communion

So Jesus said to them, "Truly, truly, I say to you, unless you eat the flesh of the Son of Man and drink His blood, you have no life in yourselves." (John 6:53)

When we read through the entire chapter of John 6 it gives us insight into why the crowds of people wanted to kill Jesus. They were incensed by the above statement because it sounded "occultish". I believe Jesus deliberately made this statement blunt to get our attention of how important it is to understand this truth. These words can either make you want to kill Jesus by turning a deaf ear or seek to understand what Jesus meant by this 'weighty' statement. Put simply...you and I cannot have any true life in ourselves if we do not eat His body and drink the blood of Christ. Could this mean once a month as most churches practice in a robotic or religious manner?

To eat of Jesus' flesh and to drink of His blood is to become partakers of His divine nature through communion. 2 Peter 1:4;

> **"For by these He has granted to us His precious and magnificent promises, so that by them you may become partakers of the divine nature, having**

escaped the corruption that is in the world by lust."

As we partake of Him we gain access to His promises through the rewiring of our Adamic DNA to the DNA of God.

Our DNA in the natural, informs medical professionals who our parents are, our blood type, any abnormalities and so on. When we are wired with the Lord or joined to the Lord we become one with Him as the Bible says in 1 Corinthians 6:17; "**...he who is joined to the Lord is one spirit with Him.**" So you see, for us to become one with the Lord we need to have His DNA. Equally so, if we are joined to negative spirits, diseases, sickness or sin, which we have partaken of through our generations, our DNA needs to be cleansed by partaking of God's DNA through communion; drinking His blood and eating His flesh.

We must also understand that like God we are three in one. We are spirit, soul and body; if we are not born of God then only our body and soul are in operation. As children of God, the DNA Jesus was given by His Heavenly Father, is given to us activating us in all three parts. As we empty ourselves and partake of Christ, by faith we are reclaiming the spirit being that we really are; where our spirit man takes the lead of our soul and body.

As human beings we attempt to nourish our bodies with natural food to help our souls, mind, will and emotion to function correctly. However, as Spirit beings we edify our spirit man so that our soul and our bodies are nourished. Which of the two are you doing? Remember we serve an inside out God.

What is communion?
According to the dictionary, the word communion is sharing or exchanging of intimate thoughts and

feelings, especially on a mental or spiritual level. 1 Corinthians 11:24-27;

> *And when He had given thanks, He broke it and said, "This is My body, which is for you; do this in remembrance of Me." In the same way He took the cup also after supper, saying, "This cup is the new covenant in My blood; do this, as often as you drink it, in remembrance of Me." For as often as you eat this bread and drink the cup, you proclaim the Lord's death until He comes. Therefore whoever eats the bread or drinks the cup of the Lord in an unworthy manner, shall be guilty of the body and the blood of the Lord.*

I believe communion is a place in our hearts that we maintain an unbroken fellowship with God; in Oneness. We can do this as many times as we eat and drink consciously. Communion is about becoming conscious of the love Jesus displayed by His life, His death, His resurrection and His ascension.

The word that Jesus used was "remembrance". That word remembrance in the Hebrew symbolises a weapon that cuts or cuts off. Hence every time we remember Christ through communion, we should visualise cutting off every illegal umbilical cord that is attempting to control us like puppets. As His body was broken, so that we could be made whole. We should pray an alignment of our souls, our bodies with our spirit man- wholeness.

Also, when we partake by faith of His body and drink of His blood, it helps us to consciously become more aware of being in Christ or abiding with Him.

Communion breaks off the religious mind-set of food being our sustainer and truly embrace the Bread of Life as the only one that satisfies. As we eat, stay in communion and remember Him through meditation. Remember what eating of His flesh is doing to our human flesh. As we eat of His flesh, we gain supernatural revelation of His Word as it breaks off wrong perceptions, wrong belief systems and brings us into a state of wholeness.

As we drink His blood, we become aware that we are being sanctified by His pure blood. We are empowered, causing divine order in our DNA, partaking of everything that is connected to the blood of Jesus and a new record of His DNA is being imprinted.

Let us commune with Him and be engrafted in Him as we seek to embrace ourselves as the spirit beings we are, emptying ourselves of all that conditions us to be human beings.

Facts are not always God's truth. Below are some FACTS (lies) I have begun to dispel because they contradict the Word of God.

Facts communion dispels

- Over 40, eyesight weakens (Isaiah 40:31).
- Metabolism will decrease if you don't eat regularly.
- Wrinkles come at a certain age.

Please note: you can have communion any time with His word through meditation; through worship; by listening to the word. Communion is God's way to assist us to stay in 24 hour connection with our Saviour. As you eat your meals you can corporate the partaking of His body and the drinking of His blood. I believe by faith you can use any type of food to represent His flesh for example as you bless your food ask the Lord to change a piece of chicken into His body and your cup of water into His blood and partake. So do not go about this religiously but endeavour to make this a lifestyle. **I encourage you to get some bread and some grape juice or wine for yourself and declare.**

Declaration

Lord Jesus you said ***"Whoever eats My flesh and drinks My blood has eternal life, and I will raise him up at the last day....He who eats My flesh and drinks My blood abides in Me, and I in him."*** *Today I choose to commune with you in a new way. I come into agreement with all that your blood represents. As I take the cup which is your blood by faith that Your DNA will begin to cleanse me of all Adamic records of generations passed. Instead I call forth a ONENESS with You that is unbroken. Lord set me apart, change me from the inside -out. Thank you for the bread, Your Body and as I consume it, I declare an enablement to overcome in all I do. Today I purpose in my heart to make You my food and to* *know in my heart that You are love. As I consume YOU I will no longer eat food out of fear of being weak or sick, but I will eat and drink of You who satisfies me physically, spiritually, emotionally and mentally. Thank You that You are my eternal life. Through You in me I too reflect the Christ in me so many will see You. Through You I speak life and see dead situations breathe life.*

Day 8:
Jesus – The Great High Priest

> *"Therefore, since we have a Great High Priest who has passed through the heavens, Jesus the Son of God, let us hold fast our confession." (Hebrews 4:14)*

In the Old Testament, Melchizedek was acknowledged as the priest of God. The priests were responsible for making intercessions to God for the people by offering sacrifices that the law required. Among the priest one was selected by the people as the High Priest, and he would enter into the Holy of Holies once a year on the Day of Atonement to place the blood of the sacrifice on the Ark of the Covenant (Hebrews 9:7). These daily and yearly sacrifices temporarily covered the sins of the people until Jesus the Messiah came to take away our sins once and for all. Like the Levitical Priests, Jesus offered a sacrifice to satisfy the Law of God when He offered Himself for our sins (Hebrews 7:26-27). Unlike the Levitical Priests, who had to continually offer sacrifices, Jesus only had to offer His sacrifice once, gaining eternal redemption for all who come to God through Him (Hebrews 9:12).

How AWESOME is that?! The sacrifice of Jesus, removed the need for a middle man or a mediator; Jesus is our only mediator. Today we still have many believers who are looking to the middle man; rather than to Jesus Himself. We would seek out our Pastors, Prophets, Apostles, Teachers, Evangelists, Pope and Priest more than we seek to spend time with our Lord. This is not to say, we do not need the fivefold ministry or people for that matter. We do, but it must always be clear that we need Jesus far much more and seek Him first. He is our Melchizedek, our Priest of God. He is always interceding for us.

In John 17 we see the Lord Jesus interceding and pouring out His heart of love for us. He shares His heart with the Father that we may be one as He and the Father are one. This is a great example of Jesus standing in the gap for us as our High Priest. He was not only praying for His disciples then, but for those to come; you and I...

Many think of the Lord's prayer as the prayer that Jesus taught His disciples to pray in Luke 11:1-4 **"Our Father who are in Heaven...."** but I believe that John 17 is the Lord's prayer. I believe if we want to know the Lord's desire for us, and the relationship He desires for us to share, then, it is all embedded in this prayer. He prayed 7 things for us, His believers:

1. To be kept from evil.
2. Unity of all believers as the Triune God are one.
3. Sanctification and separation of believers to the full work of God, as He had been set apart for His work.
4. World recognition of God's love
5. Reunion with Christ.
6. To see His glory.
7. Joy of Christ fulfilled in all believers.

We must see from this prayer that Jesus focused on being our mediator and intercessor. Jesus showed Himself as someone who stands in the gap for us. His dependency on the Father and His love for us enabled Him to pray with fluency, proficiency, clarity and accuracy.

How are we priests?

We too, have been given this ability to stand in the gap and pray for each other with prayers, groans and tongues. As we partner with the Holy Spirit to direct our prayers, praying out of love, we too will have the same results as Jesus. We are called to intercede for our nations, for our governments, for our cities, our communities, our families and our lives. As we pray and synchronize Heaven with Earth by praying the heart of the Father we will see His results. We cannot influence those we have failed to love.

Jesus being our Great High Priest is really awesome, because as a man, He was subject to all the weaknesses and temptations that we sometimes succumb to. He could personally relate to us in all our struggles (Hebrews 4:15). We have a Priest that is greater than any other priest that is why He is referred to as our "Great High Priest". He is different because He is relatable, He is holy, He dwells in the Holy of Holies and He is our intercessor. We are not going before a High Priest who will judge and condemn us, but one who invites us to come as we are and be honest with Him. He is the High Priest who covers us in prayer. Our invitation is to come boldly **"unto the throne of grace, that we may obtain mercy, and find grace and help in time of need"** (Hebrews 4:16).

As brothers and sisters of this Great High Priest we must ensure that the love and mercy that has been shown to us, we extend it to others. As our weaknesses are exposed and we battle through our temptations, we must ensure that we do not become self-righteous and condemn others in their weakness. Be sure to imitate the very heart of our Lord Jesus by praying for others and coming along side with the intention to provide guidance and support for repentance. This could be by sharing our weaknesses and the keys we have learnt that has helped us to overcome by His Grace. Nobody likes someone preaching at them, but we all endear to those who have suffered and can relate to what we are going through. We too are priest called to be like Jesus. The Bible says we are ***"a royal priesthood a people belonging to God"*** (1 Peter 2:9-10). We, like our Priest, must stand in the gap praying with '**great compassion**' like our Saviour.

Bringing our cases to the Courts of Heaven

When we think of interceding for ourselves, others or our nation; so often we think of beseeching, but the Bible reveals to us a way that is very effective.

Throughout scripture we can see Earth was patterned after Heaven. As we have armies that are sent to fight for countries so too Heaven has the heavenly host that are sent to fight for God's people.

Like Earth, there is a judicial system so too there is one in Heaven. How do I know? The Bible gives us numerous examples. Before we look at these examples: - Have you ever considered why God is referred to as Judge (Psalm 7:11)? Why Jesus is called an advocate or the executor of the will of the Father (John 17)? Or even why satan is called an accuser (Revelations 12:10)?

It is because of this judicial system. Let's lay a biblical foundation... Job 1:6-7;

> ***"Now there was a day when the sons of God came to present themselves before the Lord, and Satan also came among them. And the Lord said to satan, "From where do you come?" So satan answered the Lord and said "From the going to and from on the earth, and from walking back and forth on it."***

Also, Job 2:1;

> *"There was a day when the sons of God came to present themselves before the Lord, and satan came also among them to present himself before the Lord."*

It is interesting that the Bible describes two separate times that as the sons of God came to present themselves before the Lord so did satan. Why is he there? Zechariah 3:1;

> *"Then he showed me Joshua the high priest standing before the Angel of the Lord, and satan standing at his right hand to oppose him"*

Here we see a picture that captivates what is happening in the spirit. The enemy was there to oppose what Joshua was presenting to the courts of Heaven. The enemy satan is the accuser of the brethren. I know this because most times when I have gone to the courts I have been opposed by the enemy, through intimidation of some sort, most times he threatens my life, hoping that I will back off and give into fear. However, I have found presenting my case in the heavenly courts to be very quick and effective.

The Lord is calling us to know we are priest who can come freely into the courts of Heaven. Our enemy satan is a legalist; who accuses us night and day as it says in Revelation 12:10-12. Unfortunately not many believers have been going into the courtroom and presenting their case. We fail to realize that it is in the courtroom that permission is given to do right and wrong. This scripture tells us that we overcome because of the blood which allows us to enter the court room and by testifying as priest before our Father the judge. The enemy has been accusing us but it is time for us to destroy the works of the enemy by turning up in the courtroom.

In Luke 18:1-8 we see the story of the persistent widow that brought her case before the unjust judge. In verses 6-8 it reads;

> **"And will God not bring about justice for His chosen ones who cry out to Him day and night? Will He keep putting them off? I tell you He will see that they get justice, and quickly."**

The Lord promises that when we come into the courts and testify He WILL give us justice QUICKLY. We only need to believe Him when He says in Hebrews 4: 16 that we are to **"come boldly to the throne of grace to obtain mercy and find grace to help in time of need."** Guilt, condemnation and shame tell us that we are not good enough and that we cannot go before a holy God. So often we shrink back by pulling away our hearts from the only One who can help in our time of need. Jesus is the High Priest of our confession so the moment we confess our sin, Jesus takes it to the Father and the accuser can no longer accuse us. 1 John 1:9; **"When we confess our sin He is faithful and just to forgive us from all unrighteousness"._

When we understand that the courtroom is where we win; where we bring our issues to God and get solution; where we silence the enemy and where we come out as victors we will not give into fear for our lives, but we will come boldly before the Judge - our Father in Heaven.

How do we get into the courtroom? We enter the courts with praise (Psalm 100:4).

Declaration

As Jesus is so am I. Therefore I declare that... Jesus You are my Great High Priest, my Great Intercessor. Today, I stand in agreement to partner with You as my advocate and with our Father the judge. Psalm 100 says I enter the courts with praise and today I enter the courts shouting praises that by the blood of Jesus and my testimony that I have already overcome. I praise you that the You are a God that can never fail.

Today as Your victorious daughter, I will take my rightful place as priest to determine what goes in and what is thrown out of the courts by standing in the gap. I come presenting my case before the Judge (My Father in Heaven) shouting His praises and decreeing. Anything the accuser will use to accuse me I willingly confess (speak about those things in detail until you are empty) and I repent before my God. I declare victory in this area …….. of my life. I declare victory in this *area ……..of my ministry, I declare victory for my nation in this area……. I declare that there will be a quick manifestation of that which I have brought to the court because My Father has promised that He will answer speedily.*

Day 9:

Jesus – The Healer

> *"By His wounds you were healed"* (1Peter 2:24b)

Jesus is indeed our healer the Great Physician. When doctors are baffled and see no hope, Jesus demonstrates that healing is the children's bread. Scriptures reveal that no one came to Jesus that was not healed. Jesus broke all sabbatical laws and healed. He was renowned for healing others that many sought Him out making holes in roofs so as to get their healing, pushing through crowds just to touch the hem of His garment. Jesus was never too tired, nor was He ever too busy to heal. No sickness phased Him there was no big ones and small ones. In fact in one instance, Jesus was so confident of the Holy Spirit's power to heal He lingered in a town longer so that the dead would be buried and even begin to rot so the Father in Heaven would be glorified. Healing was one of Jesus' way of expressing His love for others. He said without a word but by His actions that He cared about what brings us pain discomfort and seeks to oppress us. What an awesome Lord!

If Jesus' relentless acts of love through healing was not enough, He left us with no doubt when He willingly hung on the cross for us. The blood of Jesus Christ bought for us salvation, our healing, deliverance, prosperity and so much more and one of His last words before He died was "it is finished". It means we need to appropriate what He has so sacrificially bought for us not plead or beg because IT IS FINISHED!!

Seeing yourself through the eyes of Jesus

When we examine the epistles, which were written for us Christians, you will see it was written in the past tense. 1 Peter 2:24 is no exception... Peter made it clear that we WERE healed by His stripes. For every slash Jesus received on His back I believe Jesus was consoling Himself, saying that it was so we can walk in complete freedom in physical, emotional and mental health.

A revelation of this reality or truth empowers us as believers to not only claim our healing but to contend for others to be healed because of the huge price that was paid for us. I know there are many who have not had this revelation. I was a Christian for 15 years and completely debilitated by fibromyalgia (arthritis in the muscles). During that period I had been to church consistently I had never heard a message on healing. My previous statement is not to blame but to show the reality of the lack of revelation of what is rightly ours. My journey was one of ignorance until...

One day I was in great despair of the life I had settled for; I had had enough. I threw myself on the carpet of my home and cried uncontrollably as I told the Lord with finality that I no longer wanted this sickness. As I did, I heard my mouth say "I would never say again that I have fibromyalgia." This bold statement could not have been mine because I had never heard a message on the power of words at this point. I had never seen someone healed supernaturally nor had a heard of any testimonies. However, these words, induced great faith in me. From that day, though I had the symptoms and pain of fibromyalgia, I stood by my confession "I was healed from fibromyalgia!" I would love to say to you that it went away the next day but it didn't. In fact, I had to take tablets for another 6 months before I noticed a change in my body. Between 6 months and a year I began see a shift and I began to notice that I did not need my medicine anymore. Soon I began to see the full manifestation of my healing. The pain disappeared the way it appeared. Since then, the pain has tried to come back many times but I made the same confession "I am healed!"

Lessons learnt from my own testimony and from releasing healing to others

1. The power of words through diagnosis and prognosis can connect you to sickness and generational illnesses
2. The power of words can invite a spirit of infirmity to attach themselves through diagnosis and prognosis
3. Unresolved emotional trauma is an open door to sickness.
4. Blatant un-forgiveness can cause infirmities emotional and mental baggage can begin to affect us physically

Lies that prevent us from experiencing the healing power of Jesus

1. The patient must have faith
2. You must pray for healing
3. The length of prayer is crucial
4. Knowing the source of the illness is crucial
5. The Father may not be in the mood to heal
6. I am not anointed to heal
7. I don't feel the anointing
8. Healing is based on how good we are
9. You have to believe in Jesus to be healed

The Bible clearly says in **Exodus 23:25-26 ....Worship the** Lord your God and His blessings will be on your food and water. I will take away sickness from among you....I will give you a full life span. Tolerating sickness or premature death is not an option. All believers are commissioned to heal the sick.... In fact, Mark 16:17-18 describes the attesting signs of the believer....

"Those who believe, in My name they will drive out demons; they will speak in new languages; They will pick up serpents; and even if they drink anything deadly, it will not hurt them; they will lay hands on the sick and they will get well."

Jesus even went a step further and promised us in John 14:12 that we would do greater works than He did. How amazing is that?!!!! This is the kind of faith He has in His ability in us, so we need to step out and begin to pray for anyone who is sick because if it does not look like Heaven, then as citizens of Heaven and Earth we should not allow it. Jesus taught us to pray that **"As it is in Heaven so it shall be on earth."**

We can bring Heaven to Earth when we believe we have access to Heaven. Jesus had an open Heaven that worked with Him, so we too have an open Heaven that works with us. The Bible says that we are to come boldly to the Throne of Grace. Therefore we have access to all that is in Heaven. Heidi Baker shares an encounter she had, where she visited Heaven and saw a room filled with different colours and shape eyes. This tells me, Heaven has body parts that we can bring to Earth. There is no sickness in Heaven. Therefore, these body parts are waiting on the sons of God to arise and use the resources that have been given to us. Consequently, we can ask Jesus to send the angels to fetch different parts of the body for those who need it.

Recently I was praying for a lady who could not see from one eye. She asked if I would pray for her. I prayed a simple prayer for the Lord to give her a new eye. After the prayer I asked "any difference?" She said "no". She then shared "I saw Jesus, He came and gave me a new eye so I believe I am healed." I decided to agree with her according to the principle of agreement in Matthew 18:19. I prayed again for the manifestation of that new eye; she began to scream and said "I can see!!" I believe she was given a new eye. I shared this testimony, to reiterate that there are body parts in Heaven, we just need to believe, act and watch Heaven merge with Earth.

The Bible says that Jesus healed them all - meaning no exceptions! He was not thwarted by how badly the disease was or how dead someone was. He healed them ALL period. We must not be moved by what we see nor what we have heard.

- Jesus wants people in their right minds (2 Timothy 1:7)
- loss of muscle power - no condition is hopeless John5:6;
- Jesus healed the oppressed because God was with Him (Acts 10:38);

- Diverse diseases (Isaiah 61:1, Luke 4:18) ulcers, diabetes, heart problems, cancer.

Bottom line, no sickness is too big... He is able! He only asks that we believe His word and step out and believe.

Declaration

Acts 10:38 says God anointed Jesus of Nazareth with the Holy Ghost and with power; who went about doing good, and healing all that were oppressed of the devil; for God was with him. So because as Jesus is so am I... I declare that God anointed me ....(your name) with the Holy Ghost and with power; and as I go out I do good by healing all that are oppressed of the devil; for God is SURELY with me.

Day 10:

Jesus – The Prophet

> *"Surely the Lord God does nothing, unless He reveals His secret counsel to His servants the prophets." (Amos 3:7)*

The Bible teaches several roles of the prophet. The prophet is to edify, exhort and encourage the Saints. The prophet aligns the Saints according to the purposes of God. Ultimately, the prophet's role is to bring the heart of man back to the Father. A prophet can do that in many ways by foretelling, forth telling or by disclosing a fact about the persons present or past; this is referred to as a word of knowledge. A word of wisdom, which is a directional word.

We see Jesus in the role of prophet in John 4:19 when He met the Samaritan woman. He downloaded from His Father in Heaven, a profound word of knowledge about the Samaritan's life. Jesus said in verse 18 of John 4 **"you have had five husbands, and the one whom you now have is not your husband".** This prophetic word, in turn helped the Samaritan to not only face the truth of her life, but to come to true repentance before God and man. She was so repentant before man that when she told the villagers her testimony they too came to know Jesus personally.

In John 1:47 we see another profound example of Jesus speaking into the life of Nathanael. Jesus was able to see Nathanael and to download information from Heaven about his character. Jesus said **"here is an Israelite indeed (a true descendant of Jacob), in whom there is no guile nor deceit nor falsehood nor duplicity!"** Jesus revealed to

Nathaniel his heritage; that He was a true Israelite. He also spoke about his character; the honesty and integrity that Nathanael exuded.

Nathanael was so amazed at the prophecy of Jesus he asked the Lord, "How do you know me? How is it that you know these things about me?" By the very prophecy of Jesus, Nathanael was able to identify immediately the reality of who Jesus was; that He was a Teacher, the Son of God, the King of Israel. By Nathanael's confession of who Jesus was, he entrusted his heart and belief in Jesus as Lord. This is a testimony of Jesus being a prophet and how by His grace people were able to give their hearts back to the Father.

We too can be prophetic like Jesus. As we were made in His image; as He is so are we. In Luke 21:14-15 Jesus actually gives us some tips about how to flow in the prophetic. He says;

"Make up your minds not to prepare beforehand to defend yourselves; for I will give you utterance and wisdom which none of your opponents will be able to resist or refute."

HALLELUJAH!! The Lord is encouraging us not to make up our minds on what we will say because it prevents Him from using us as His mouthpiece. However, when we surrender our mouths and flow with Him, He will give us words that will leave those who oppose us in awe of God and an inability to disprove His power. This scripture also implies, the need to trust and be courageous; two important characteristics needed to flow in the prophetic. When we fill our minds with what we will say, it leaves no room to for us to download what the Lord is saying. This will mean trusting that as you open your mouth He will give you the words. Also, when those words come, do not analyse; be bold and speak without editing despite their facial expressions

Jesus Himself told us in John10:4-5 **"The sheep follow him because they know his voice. A stranger he simply will not follow, but will flee from him."** This tells me that the prophetic flows out of an intimate relationship with God, because I will only know the voice of someone I speak to or commune with regularly. When you are in constant communion with the person of God the Father, Son, and Holy Ghost, your ear becomes more attuned to His voice. If we claim to be children of God then we should know the voice of our Daddy. If a child came and told you they did not know their Dad's voice we would assume they do not know their Dad. The same is true in spiritual matters.

The prophet not only hears but sees and uses all their physical senses to download what

God is saying. This is in our DNA because we are one with Christ and we no longer live, but Christ lives in us. Therefore, as long as we are in the spirit we are able to see, feel and sense all Papa God is feeling. . God has proven this to me numerous times.

On a few occasions, someone will ask me to seek God for a friend in prayer that I don't know. I will ask God for a picture, anything that He wants to highlight. Well since I know nothing about this person, it helps me to be completely abandoned. Most times instantaneously I get a picture of the person. In many instances I can describe the person's physical appearance. God will sometimes allow me to feel pain in areas of my body where they are having pains and sometimes I have been told the name of their illness. Sometimes He will give me a word of wisdom which helps to direct the person to bring breakthrough. Many will read this testimony and say, "it is because you are gifted", but what we fail to see is that we are all gifted. We all need to come to the realisation that we have God on the inside of us and so everything we need to know is in Him. In Proverbs 20:12 it says; "**Ears to hear and eyes to see—both are gifts from the LORD.**" we simply need to ask the Lord for the ability to see and hear in the spirit.

In Ezekiel 12:12;

> **"Son of man, you are living among a rebellious people. They have eyes to see but do not see and ears to hear but do not hear, for they are a rebellious people."**

This scripture implies that it is a heart hardened by rebellion that prevents us from hearing and seeing. The Bible is clear that God wants to have an intimate relationship with us; if we are not able to communicate in a dialogue it would be a lopsided relationship.

Though we are aware, all of God's children should be able to prophesy because this gift is birthed out of relationship; we acknowledge that there are some that our God has empowered and called to sit in the office of the Prophet, but that is different to the ability to prophesy.

The Bible says in Psalms 139:18 "***if I could count them (referring to His thoughts) they would outnumber the sand.***" That tells me that Papa God is always thinking of me. It also tells me that we can ask Him for a word for anyone and Papa God will have something to say. I have been to numerous services where only five people in the congregation are prophesied over and I assumed it was because God had nothing to say to the others. From this scripture it tells me God is never out of words, He is always sharing His heart with us; we

only need to be sensitive to the numerous ways in which He speaks. He speaks to us:-
- Through random thoughts
- An impression
- Being drawn to something
- Pictures
- Songs
- Repetition

How do we receive prophetic words from the Lord?

1. Declutter your thoughts
2. Ask the Lord for a picture, a word, a thought concerning the person or yourself.
3. Ask Him for the interpretation (if you do not understand)
4. Begin to speak it out or write what you saw or hear. You will find as you step out to share the picture develops or you begin to hear more; just flow.

I encourage you to expect Papa God to speak to you anytime, anyplace and almost immediately when you ask Him a question. When you have heard Him, step out and share what you are hearing in humility. I usually begin by saying something of the sort…."I sense or I perceive…." and then I ask if what I said resonates in any way. As Jesus is so are you; so prophesy.

Declaration

God is my Daddy. I am one with Him, therefore what He sees, hears, feels, smells, I can have access to it, because I am one with Him. I am prophetic because Jesus is prophetic and He is my pattern. My ears are attentive to the voice of the Lord and I am quick to obey not reason away His voice. So I say, speak Lord for your servant is listening.

Day 11:
Jesus – The Teacher

> *"Truly, truly, I say to you, we speak of what we know and testify of what we have seen, and you do not accept our testimony. If I told you earthly things and you do not believe, how will you believe if I tell you heavenly things?"*
> *(John 3:11-13)*

As a trained teacher, I am completely captivated by Jesus and the way He went about teaching. Everywhere He went people were often amazed at His teachings, the wisdom He emanated, His profound way of thinking and His unique way of seeing situations left many speechless. For others, His views challenged, evoked feelings of dismay as it sought to transform the thoughts of others.

Jesus demonstrated that being a teacher is not the transferring of information or facts rather imparting or releasing transformation to others. This is not always by articulating but in many forms of communication. Jesus was not only the WORD; He is the Word that became flesh, which is crucial for us too....What do I mean by this? When we allow the word to become flesh through meditating and applying, the word becomes spirit in us and can be imparted to others through us.

We see an excellent example of this in the book of John chapter 3. The Bible tells us of a man named Nicodemus who came to Jesus, who was considered by the people of that time the ruler of the Jews. Nicodemus recognised Jesus as a Rabbi or a Teacher. He knew that no man could do these miracles unless they were from God. In other words, Nicodemus' definition of a teacher was someone who not only taught but whose actions backed up their teaching. You see the miracles testified the truth of Jesus' teaching. 1 Corinthians 4:20 says it this way **"For the kingdom of god does not consist in words but in power".**

Jesus explained to Nicodemus that a born again experience or transformation must occur before one can become a teacher. Nicodemus being a teacher himself knew that his own teaching did not have the same effect as Jesus'. He saw that Jesus' teaching left people changed. In John 3:9 Nicodemus was perplexed by Jesus statement of being born again and inquired of the Lord. But...the Lord inquired of him in verses 10 and 11;

> **"Are you the teacher of Israel and you do not understand these things? Truly, truly, I say to you, we speak of what we know and testify of what we have seen, and you do not accept our testimony."**

Jesus was amazed that Nicodemus did not understand the concept of being born again and he was called a teacher or a Rabbi. Jesus went on to point out a clear distinction between His teaching and Nicodemus' teaching. His teaching was from experiential knowledge, things that He Himself had encountered, while it is implied that Nicodemus teaching was mere information. Jesus revealed the secret as to why His teaching caused transformation in others; He clearly told Nicodemus it was because He lived what He taught.

We also see that because of this truth, Jesus did not need to teach for people to be healed, delivered, or raised from the dead. In some cases He just spoke the word and was not even at the place where the healing occurred. In other cases some touched Him and they were healed. I believe this was a testimony of this truth He spoke to Nicodemus, that when the word is lived, applied or becomes flesh then power is infused and imparted to others directly and indirectly.

What are the ways Jesus taught?

- Stories in the forms of parables
- Capitalising on teachable moments (Matthew 13 with the woman being stoned is an excellent example).
- No matter how tired He was He always made time for the people.
- He never watered down the truth
- He used the time allotted to Him well by cutting to the chase rather than being longwinded
- He asked rhetorical questions, which allowed people to assess their motives and attitudes
- He used miracles to teach - miracles gave dignity and importance to those who would normally be overlooked. E.g. of the blind man calling out for help.

The World's Teaching	**Jesus' Teaching**
Strive to be the best	The first shall be last….those who exalt themselves will be emptied
Identity comes from family, name, colour wealth, career	identity comes from a relationship with God
Sinners are to be outcast and rejected	Everyone is welcomed and accepted
A Person's worth is measured by social standards (education, success…)	Our worth is invaluable, like Christ
God is angry and judgemental	God is loving and gracious
Preserve your life above all else	Dying to self leads to an abundant life

How can we be like Jesus?

As Jesus is so are we. Although some have been called to sit in the office of a teacher in the body of Christ, we are called to teach in some way. How do I know? Jesus' last words to us Matthew 28:18-20 were **"Go and make disciples of all nations."** To make disciples we need to teach.

If that were not sufficient, the Bible says in 2 Timothy 2:15;

> **"Be diligent to present yourself approved to God, as a workman who does not need to be ashamed, accurately handling the word of truth."**

2 Timothy 4:2;

> **"Preach the word in season and out of season, reprove, rebuke, exhort with great patience and instruction."**

Colossians 4:6;

> *"Let your speech always be with grace, as though seasoned with salt, so that you will know how to respond to each person."*

Only with His words in our heart are we able speak with grace. 1 Peter 3:15 tells us to **"always be prepared to give an answer to everyone....and be ready to return a defence to everyone who requests a statement from you about the hope of your faith."** So you see, we should aim to be a teacher like Jesus by giving an answer for what we believe.

In order to teach like Jesus we must capture the heart and mind-set of our Lord. We must choose to embrace His teachings by meditating on His words and allowing them to become flesh so that we are not just hearers but doers as well.

Declaration

I declare like Jesus that I am not a giver of information. Like Jesus the words I speak are life. The Life of Jesus is imparted into others because the WORD has become FLESH in me. I declare that I too am from God; as God is with me miracles will accompany all the teachings that the Holy Spirit will lead me to impart.

Day 12:

Jesus – Lion of Judah

> *"Judah is a lion's whelp; From the prey, my son, you have gone up. He crouches, he lies down as a lion, And as a lion, who dares rouse him up?" (Genesis 49:9)*

The lion is perceived as the king of the jungle. The king of jungle rules and dominates all the other animals. Jesus is called the King of kings. Like the lion we are called to be vigilant and alert in the spirit; to see clearly, to hear distant sounds and know the direction in which our enemy is coming.

There are three facets of the Lion of Judah I would like to highlight. His roar, His rest and His reign.

<u>Lions roar</u>

In Matthew 27:46 the Bible describes Jesus at the end of His gruelling journey of the cross, crying out to the Father. Scripture reveals that throughout this journey He did not defend Himself, nor tried to justify His actions. In fact, this is the first time throughout His journey that He cried out... ***in a loud voice He said "Eli, Eli, Lama, Sabachthani?" that is "My God, My God, why have You forsaken ME?"*** The Bible said Jesus cried out again and gave up His Spirit. Here is an example of Jesus roaring as the Lion of Judah.

The Bible points out that after He roared four things happened:-

1. The veil of the temple was torn in two from top to bottom.
2. The earth shook.
3. The rocks were split.
4. The tombs were opened and many bodies of the saints who had fallen asleep were raised.

These four extraordinary events carry tremendous application. The veil is the fabric that was used to separate us from coming boldly into the throne room of God. Like Jesus, when we speak, sing or pray, as we are prompted by the Holy Spirit, we are roaring and anything that has prevented others from coming into the Holy of Holies can be removed by faith. I understand this as removing anything in the atmosphere that is acting as a deterrent in the spirit.

The shaking of the earth and the rocks splitting is just that, a shaking up. An experience that does not leave you the same. It leaves you with the fear of God all over you. A feeling of awe and wonder at the amazing God we serve. The roar leaves an indelible mark on you. When a rock split or crack, even if you endeavour to glue the pieces together, the broken marks would still be shown. In the same way, you will never be the same after that roar; it will mark you forever.

The tombs were opened, and many bodies of the Saints who had fallen asleep were raised. This reality endorsed the truth of John 11:26 where Jesus said; **"everyone who lives and believes in Me will never die."** Here the resurrection power of Jesus is demonstrated. This roar was so powerful it breathed life into dead bodies that were fallen asleep (dead). The Bible says in Proverbs 18:21 that the power of life and death are in the tongue. This is a powerful demonstration of what happens when the roar of God is released through us, anything that was dead spiritually (dreams, goals and longings) must be awakened. A spiritual and a physical awakening occurs after this roar.

An important point to note is that the roar, when prompted by the Holy Spirit, is the sound of Heaven. When this sound is released these things must happen. I believe the prophetic word, when released, does these four things as outlined above. When we are cognizant that our words act as a roar from Heaven, we become more mindful; endeavouring that our words are spirit and life as Jesus' (John 6:63). Let us speak, sing, shout and prophesy as the spirit prompts, so we can tap into, the power of the roar. HALLELUJAH!!!

Lion's rest
Mark 6:31 says;

> ***And Jesus said to them, "Come away by yourselves to a secluded place and rest a while." (For there were many***

people coming and going, and they did not even have time to eat.).

Here we see Jesus encouraging us to separate time for Him as we find our rest in Him and to declutter our minds and hearts.

A lion is said to sleep for 20 hours a day. Like the lion, Jesus invites us to rest in Him. God Himself rested on the seventh day from all His works; this implies that the Lion understood the concept of peace. The Bible says in Colossians 3:15 that we should **"let peace be the umpire of our faith."** That is, we should allow peace to assist us in making decisions. Sovereign acts of God, miracles and divine strategies are given when we rest.

In Psalm 46:10 the Bible says; **"Be still and know that I am God"**. This Scripture points out that there is a revelation knowledge, wisdom and understanding in times of being still. Adam, Jacob, and Samuel were sleeping when God did miracles in their lives. Adam received Eve, Jacob received his promise and Samuel received instructions; this all happened as they rested. When we rest, God will put things together for us; you can receive strategy, insight, promises, comfort, and more! So take time to rest. It takes faith to enter His rest. Anxiety, worry and fear are all deterrent factors that prevent us from resting. Have you noticed when our sleep is broken, we wake up, feeling tired and in pain. Striving tells us that we need to figure it out, while faith reassures us of God's faithfulness.

The word 'rest' is synonymous to the word 'peace'. This is particularly significant because we see Jesus in the midst of the storm calling the storm peace. He used peace or rest to calm the storm by calling the storm what He wanted it to be. He said **"Peace be still"** not "Storm be still".

This is a great example of calling the things that are not as though they were. Undoubtedly, it demonstrates the reality that to have peace is to have power. We see from the words that Jesus spoke, that He did not see the storm as something to be afraid of, because He knew He had the power of peace within, to calm any storm.

"Blessed are the peacemakers for they are the sons of God." (Matthew 5:9)

In John 8:1, Jesus bent down and wrote while the Pharisees were trying to accuse and condemn the woman caught in adultery. Jesus kept His peace by getting the Pharisees to assess themselves by using reverse psychology... **"He who has no sin let him throw the first stone."** Sometimes when we feel attacked and condemned by people's words, it is easy to react rashly, but Jesus sets us a great example of how to respond by helping our accusers to evaluate their own actions.

Another example that comes to mind is when Jesus was nailed to the cross. It would have been very easy to become self-piteous and angry with the pain He had to endure, but instead of focusing on Himself He focused on others. He ensured His Mum was taken care of and graciously led one of the thieves into salvation. Again a lesson to deal with those who persecute you and treat you unfairly; don't focus on yourself but on helping others. God will sort out your persecutors and most importantly you will keep your peace.

Peace is not just the absence of war. It is the presence of inexplicable tranquillity, completion and wholeness in the midst of turmoil. To live in His Presence is to live in peace.

Lion as ruler

The lion as a ruler, suggests stepping into the role as a lord. God is the Lord of lords; we are that lower case lord. God has stipulated a law that requires Him to have an ambassador on earth to partner with - without this partnership, He is limited. He stipulated this law because He desired to be ONE with man. Hence why we must understand what a lord is and what a lord does in order to reclaim our lordship.

Lordship suggests ownership and therefore rulership. Jesus being The Lord of all lords means there is no other authority. He reigns over all things; He is absolute and sacred. God raised Him from the dead and placed Him over all things.

*"**Far above all rule and authority and power and dominion, and above every name that is named, not only in this age but also the age to come. All things***

were put under His feet and God gave Him head over all things to the church, which is his body, the fullness of him who fills all in all." (Ephesians 1:21-23)

Rulers are not beggars:-
1. Stop asking for what you already have.
2. Stop asking and declare what you want.
3. Speak what you want not what your circumstance dictate.
4. Embrace your lordship

Declaration

As He is so am I. So I declare that the Lion of Judah lives on the inside of me. I declare like the Lion I am a warrior of God. I carry God's creative ability, so as I roar and speak as Jesus speaks, atmospheres change, new doors are opened, the dead are raised. I declare that Jesus is my Peace and like He does, I choose to declare what I want despite not what my circumstances dictate. I declare that I am a lord and I possess the Kingdom of God. I surrender to the peace of God to reign in my life. I abandon myself in Him for He is my provision, my power, my purpose. In Him I rest. I declare that as I rule over my inheritance that the wisdom of God is my guide. I declare that I will use my blessings to exhort, edify and encourage. I declare that I will allow no-one to steal my peace by giving them my power. Instead I will rule and reign.

Day 13:

Jesus – Author and Finisher

> *"Fixing our eyes on Jesus the Author and Perfecter of our faith….." (Hebrews 12:2)*

So often we view Jesus as the author but we forget He is also the finisher. When I read this scripture I was intrigued by the word 'fix'! The word fix suggest to me glued or single-minded focus. Don't just believe He is the Author or the Finisher but look out for Him by faith to finish what He began. The day I received this revelation was the day I realised that Jesus does not expect me to carry the burden of finishing what He has instructed me to do, by myself. He wants me to lean on Him; draw strength from Him and actively believe and expect Him to finish what He has started or prompted me to do as He continues to guide, make a way, open doors for His purpose to be fulfilled. Wipe the sweat off your brow. Phew! Isn't that AWESOME!?

In Revelation John writes at the beginning and at the end of this illuminating book that Jesus is the Alpha (Aleph) and Omega (Tav); we know this means the first and the last. In the ancient Hebrew the symbol for the Aleph (ALPHA) is a cross and Tav (OMEGA) is symbolic of an ox head. To look to Jesus as the Alpha is to remind ourselves of the cross of Jesus Christ and what was purchased on our behalf. Jesus as Omega is to remember Christ, as the ox- our burden bearer, releasing all to Him that can cause us to worry. Therefore while waiting for His expected end we need to be cognisant **"to be anxious for NOTHING"** (Philippians 4:6).

Fear is the reason why we try to take the reins and attempt to carry a burden that was never ours to carry. Ask the Holy Ghost to reveal any fear that has driven your life...Ask Him to reveal the fault lines in your life so that you can experience the Lord as both the Alpha and the Omega.

Being able to see from His perspective (a panoramic view to see the end) feeds our faith to bring things to completion. It is important to have God's perspective on all things because His power flows down and not up. To receive Christ and everything God has for us, requires us to be continuously empty by admitting our inability to satisfy our deepest needs; all the while believing in the finished work of Christ. Walking in this humility, obedience and faith will attract God's gifts and His blessings.

Lord I need your grace to empty myself of all that opposes your Presence. I repent of self-

reliance that stops me from trusting You. I pray for the wisdom, peace, and power to serve You in a way that will fulfil Your purpose for my life.

To believe in the Alpha and Omega is to know undoubtedly that the good work He begun in your salvation, marriage, children, career; He will bring it to completion. This belief will lead you and I to surrender every aspect of our lives to Him by making the decision to rely on Him to finish what He has begun.

Jesus Himself said "He that has seen me has seen the Father." I believe when Jesus says I am the Alpha and Omega, He is saying He is God's signature; He carries the mark of God. Jesus is God the Father's covenant with us, His signature. To have Jesus is to have God's contract signed, sealed and approved of.

It is important to note that though Jesus is the first and the last, He is also A-Z and all the letters in between. He *was* and *is* to come. The problem is not usually with the beginning nor the end but going through the process and ensuring we are not galloping like a horse when we should be resting in Him. The ability to discern what season we are in while we go through the process will determine if we will have God's desired outcome.

Kris Volloton opened my eyes to see seasons in Psalm 23. In verse 2 'lie in green pastures' is a period where everything is bliss. A period of rest, to be still and know that God is God by walking in peace. During this period it is important we recognised that we should lie, not run ahead of God. The fruit of this position is peace.

In verse 4 we see that you walk through the valley of death and fear no evil. During this season we should walk. If we were to remain still when you are in a fire it would engulf you. So it is during these times of darkness and hardships, you can't feed discouragement and disappointment, instead, avoid feelings of apathy and self-pity. We do this by encouraging ourselves; focusing on the staff that guides and reminds us that we are not alone but God is with us. We must walk not run, because to run could mean we will miss those important landmarks that God will use to take us to the next level. Walk knowing that the rod of discipline is there to do in us that which is needed for Christ to do through us.

In verse 5 we can see that God prepares a table before us in the presence of our enemies. In this season the position necessary is to be seated. This table is laden with the Lords blessings for us to partake. We are able to sit because we know it is not because of anything we did but because of His grace. Those who mocked us and scoffed during our times of hardships will undoubtedly see the anointing of God that has so filled us that it is now overflowing to affect others. Before you can be filled you must be empty of self-effort. For you to overflow your receptacle or container has to be overfilled by partaking.

Inevitably it is important to note that the choices we make during the process will determine the end. The Israelites in the wilderness are a classic example. God wants us to follow His initiation to begin but He wants His end to come to fruition.

Jesus being Alpha and Omega in our lives means:-
1. Complete dependence
2. Absence of worry and anxiety; presence of trust
3. Walking in His peace

Examples of those in the Bible who started well but lost their way.

1. The example of Lot having God's beginning and how He lost His way in the process and missed the Lord's perfect will. (Genesis 13, 14,19)
2. King Saul who started as a great king but became proud and fell from God's grace. He allowed jealousy to cloud his judgement and did not fulfil His destiny as a result. (1 Samuel 18)
3. Samson too started well, but never dealt with the sin of lust being a snare. This same lust of his eyes, prevented him to fulfil his divine call. He disclosed the very secret that God asked him to keep regarding his strength. His lack of discretion was motivated by the lust which cost him everything (Judges 16).

Examples of those in the Bible who experienced themselves as Alpha and Omega.

1. Moses time travelled to the past and wrote the book of Genesis even though He was not born then.
2. The Apostle John was translated to the future so that on his return He could write the book of Revelation.
3. Both John and Moses wrote about their deaths in third person.

An example of being the Alpha:

I was in the kitchen washing the dishes. I was worshipping and talking to the Lord about a friend who was coming to see me the next day. He shared with me that she needed deliverance. Having witnessed so many deliverances where people threw up or puked. I asked if this were the kind of deliverance that would occur. He said *"No, this is a deliverance of one's mind being renewed."*

I somehow saw this is as a chance to speak to the Lord again about a situation that had caused me much pain. The circumstances caused me to feel overlooked and side-lined feelings of oppression became more evident. I asked the Lord why I had to go through that heartache. I was brought back to the beginning of when I was saved how I was overlooked then too. He then brought me back to the present and made me aware of how He uses me now to prophesy or to call forth His divine assignments and plans for others. The pain that I had felt when others overlooked me is to remind me never to allow selfishness to prevent me from calling out the gold in others. The pain I had in my heart for about three years instantly left that night at the sound of those words because for the first time I saw the purpose of the pain and how God could use my pain to help others.

An example of being the Omega:-

More recently, I was preparing for a missionary trip to Jamaica. The Lord had made it clear He was sending me. As we sought to arrange speaking engagements with churches, I felt that there was a lot of resistance from the enemy. The lack of breakthrough caused me to doubt the mission.

One evening I was feeling aggravated because the doors refused to open, when I inquired of the Lord about what the problem was, or more specifically I said "Lord what am I dealing with?" Instantly I found myself suspended in the sky over Jamaica and immediately saw an angel as tall as a skyscraper (since I was up in the sky and I could only see his chest (it seemed he was that tall). I believe this is the angel that has been assigned over Jamaica. He wore medals on his chest which suggested to me that he had fought many battles and was victorious. He then showed me a dark cloud which hovered over Jamaica and I instantly knew it was the spirit of religion. I sensed that this spirit was acting as an oppressor to the Jamaican people. I began to partner with the angel and prayed against the spirit of religion, when in an instant the picture changed. Soon I saw myself in front of a door and saw what seemed like an explosion of the door as it busted up into smithereens. I knew from what I had witnessed, that the Lord had again showed me the end.

To God be the glory on my arrival to Jamaica my itinerary was compact and every door the Lord instructed me to knock opened just like that door which busted in smithereens. This was a direct result of God showing me what was taking place in the spiritual realms and partnering with the angelic resources He gave me to do it. You see because we have the mark of God on our lives we too can travel in the spirit to see the end, so we can partner with the Spirit of God and align ourselves with what Heaven is doing. Jesus is the Alpha and

Omega and so are we. There are no limitations in Christ. He knows the beginning to the end. He wants to share with you the end, so that you can go through the hindrances with confidence.

Declaration

Thank You Lord that all truth is published in You. All that I need to know, I have access to because greater is He in me than He that is in the world. I declare today that every access you have given me will not be a theory of the believer's authority, but that I will practically execute the reality of this truth by expecting to know what I need to know at the right time. Today I declare that as Jesus is the Alpha and the Omega, I too have access to know the beginning and the end because Jesus lives in me.

Beloved I pray this book blessed you the way it blessed me. Continue to reclaim your identity and actively live out the REAL you in your everyday life. Be blessed. Shalom.

QUESTIONS?
Contact us @ Christine Nelson Ministries

Website:
www.christinenelson.org

Email:
christinenelsonministries@outlook.com

SIGN UP TO OUR ONLINE SUPERNATURAL CLASSES @
www.christinenelson.org/epic-supernatural

Biography

Christine Nelson is first a daughter of the Most High. Her walk with God is her shield and refuge. She is a wife to Omowale Nelson and a mother to Kobi and Kristian Nelson.

Christine is the founder of 'Christine Nelson Ministries', 'Epic Supernatural School' and 'EPIC Academy'. She has authored 3 books in the Walking in Oneness series and this is the third in the series with more to come...

She is a radio and television host for 'Revealing the Christ in you' on Tropical FM.

The Lord uses Christine as a prophetic mouthpiece and as a teacher of His word. She ministers internationally and host her own 'Walking in Oneness' retreats and conferences.

Made in the USA
Charleston, SC
15 March 2015